DENIERS OF THE HOLOCAUST

DENIERS

OF THE

HOLOCAUST

WHO THEY ARE • WHAT THEY DO • WHY THEY DO IT

Ted Gottfried

Illustrations by Stephen Alcorn

THE HOLOCAUST
Twenty-First Century Books
Brookfield, Connecticut

Chapter opening illustrations and design by Stephen Alcorn © www.alcorngallery.com

Photographs courtesy of Harry S. Truman Library/U. S. Army Signal Corps.: p. 14;
© Reuters NewMedia Inc./Corbis: p. 27; AP/Wide World Photos: pp. 40, 71, 97;
Archive Photos: pp. 46, 65 (Hulton Getty), 82 (Reuters/Jim Bourg)

Library of Congress Cataloging-in-Publication Data
Gottfried, Ted.
Deniers of the holocaust: who they are, what they do, why they do it / Ted Gottfried ;
illustrations by Stephen Alcorn.
p. cm. — (The Holocaust)
Includes bibliographical references (p.) and index.
ISBN 0-7613-1950-6 (lib. bdg.)
1. Holocaust denial—Juvenile literature. [1.Holocaust denial.]
I. Alcorn, Stephen. ill. II. Title. III. Holocaust (Brookfield, Conn.)
D804.355 .G68 2001
940.53'18—dc21   00-051221

Published by Twenty-First Century Books
A Division of The Millbrook Press, Inc.
2 Old New Milford Road
Brookfield, Connecticut 06804
www.millbrookpress.com

In memory of my mother,
Jennie Bach Gottfried
—Peace and Love

ACKNOWLEDGMENTS

I am grateful to personnel of the Judaica Room of the New York Central Research Library, the Mid-Manhattan Library, the Jewish Museum, and the Society Library in New York, and the United States Holocaust Memorial Museum in Washington, D.C., for their aid in gathering material for this book. Thanks are also due librarian Susan Rosner of the Simon Wiesenthal Center in Los Angeles for her gracious and prompt cooperation. Also, gratitude and much love to my wife, Harriet Gottfried, who—as always—read and critiqued this book. Her help was invaluable, but any shortcomings in the work are mine alone.

—Ted Gottfried

CONTENTS

Truth exists, only falsehood has to be invented.[1]

—Georges Braque

here are two sides to every argument. However, the two sides are not always equal in truth, motive, or goodwill. Sometimes it is a matter of reality versus propaganda, of fact distorted by malice, of history challenged by bigotry and hatred. To ignore the challenge, however, is to risk the rewriting of history toward monstrous ends. In the case of the Holocaust, it is to deny the massacre of millions, and the possibility of the murder of millions more.

The Holocaust

Holocaust is the name given to the genocide of European Jews in World War II. Others died in the deliberate slaughter of noncombatants—Russian prisoners of war, Polish slave laborers, Gypsies, homosexuals, and more—but none in as great numbers as the Jews. Six million Jewish civilians—men, women, children, and old people—were killed by the Nazis and their collaborators. The victims included an estimated 3,000,000 Jews from Poland, 900,000 from the Ukraine, 450,000 from Hungary, 300,000 from Romania, 228,000 from the Baltic countries, 210,000 from Germany and Austria, 105,000 from the Netherlands, 90,000 from France, 75,000 from Slovakia, and approximately half a million from the other countries of Europe. They constituted two thirds of the Jews of Europe, 90 percent of the Jews of Poland and Lithuania, one out of every three Jews in the world. The Nazis called it the Final Solution.[2]

The Final Solution was enforced by a variety of methods. Some Jews were literally worked to death. Some died of deliberate starvation. Some froze to death in the unheated dwellings of the ghettos to which they were confined by the Nazis. Jewish families were loaded into sealed vans and asphyxiated by carbon monoxide. Thousands of Jews were rounded up and murdered in mass shootings, which went on for hours, even days. Some were herded into synagogues and other buildings that were doused with gasoline and set ablaze; those who tried to escape were fired upon with machine guns until all the Jews were dead.

Jews died of sicknesses like dysentery and tuberculosis, diseases resulting from the horrendous conditions in the concentration camps where they were held. Some died particularly painful deaths as the result of medical experimentation in these camps. Half or more of the Jews who perished in the Holocaust were choked to death by the fumes released by Zyklon-B crystals in the gas chambers of the extermination camps.

Sources of Evidence

Few events in history are as well documented as the Holocaust. Contrary to their reputation, the Nazis were often sloppy in carrying out the killings. However, they were meticulous when it came to keeping records of them.

In the extermination camps they kept "Death Books," daily records of the gassing of Jews.[3] These, along with signed orders for mass executions, periodic efficiency reports on the increase in production of dead Jews, gruesome day-by-day accounts of the effects of medical experimentation on inmates, transportation records for boxcar loads of victims, invoices for the Zyklon-B crystals used to kill them, orders and bills for forklifts and furnaces used to dispose of the bodies, photographs and motion pictures taken of the murders by death-camp jailers, and hundreds of other Holocaust-related Nazi documents add up to a remarkably complete chronicle of genocide. The "full set of minutes" of the

Nazis' conference at Wannsee, a suburb of Berlin, in January 1942, spell out the plans for stepping up the Final Solution and making Europe *Judenrein*—rid of Jews.[4]

The extent to which the plan was successful is borne out by forty-two volumes of testimony from the Nazi war crimes trials held after World War II ended. Many of those who testified, confirming the slaughter, were Nazis who claimed to have just been following orders. There were also horrifying eyewitness accounts from Holocaust survivors, both during the trials and in statements recorded by journalists, United Nations interviewers, and Jewish archivists and historians. Pictures taken of both survivors and corpses by the liberating armies testify both to the mass murder and disease and starvation in the camps. Allied medical personnel and other witnesses described the evidence of maltreatment and genocide that they found. Finally, there are the mass graves created by American grave-digging machines faced with the problem of disposing of the bones of thousands of corpses.

The Language of Bigotry

Despite the overwhelming evidence, there are those who deny the Holocaust. They say that the genocide never happened. At the same time, they accept the bigotry used to justify the slaughter. In a way, this is more frightening than their denial of the Holocaust. It is the threat identified by philosopher George Santayana when he wrote that "those who cannot remember the past are condemned to repeat it."[5]

The key word which motivated the Holocaust and which drives its present-day deniers is anti-Semitism (hatred of Jews). It is an attitude based on fear and prejudice. The fear is common to many people. They are afraid of those who are different from them. The difference may be cultural, racial, or religious. The victims may be blacks, Asians, Serbs, Croats, Sikhs, Hindus, Muslims, or American Indians. Or they may be Jews.

Rows of bodies fill the yard of the Lagernordhausen concentration camp in Germany. This picture was taken by a member of the United States Army Signal Corps at the close of World War II.

Hatred becomes acceptable when one group is denied the common humanity claimed by the other group. The language of bigotry is born of this attitude. The words deprive the group, or the person, of dignity and respect, and what is left is perceived as less than human.

Calling Jews "kikes" or "hebes" or "sheenies" is buying into the myth that they are inferior. The myth feeds on itself as it grows. Rumor is accepted first as fact and then as a group characteristic. Pretty soon all members of the group are assumed to have the same loathsome traits. Pretty soon it is believed that all Jews are wretched, dirty, wily, money-hungry, rich, Communist, and plotting to take over the world. It is rumored that Jews conspire with Satan and drink the blood of non-Jewish children. No charge is too fantastic or contradictory to be believed. Jews—as the myths build and congeal with time—are capable of anything. When that happens it is all too easy for those who believe the myths to move from prejudice to persecution.

A History of Persecution

Anti-Semitism has a long history. In ancient times, during the Roman conquest of the Jewish states of Israel and Judah, the Jews were enslaved, and then they rebelled. In A.D. 132, the Romans killed more than half a million Jewish men. In A.D. 641, when Arab Muslims drove out the Romans, Jews were persecuted, and many fled the region. Many more fled anti-Semitic rampages by the Crusaders in the eleventh century.

Initially, they fled to Spain. During the Spanish Inquisition, when they had to choose between converting to Catholicism or being burned at the stake, many Jews fled to Italy, France, and Germany. In the fifteenth and sixteenth centuries they were banished from France and Portugal and migrated to Germany, and then farther east. In Germany, Poland, Russia, and other countries, Jews were made to live in segregated ghettos. Up to and throughout the nineteenth century, they were persecuted in a variety of ways.

Usually, when Jews arrived, the land in these countries was already owned. Peasants tended the crops, and there was little need for more farmworkers. Laws were passed that applied only to Jews. They could not move about freely and had to return to the ghettos before dark. They could not own land or property. They could not join craftsmen's guilds, and so could not work as carpenters, blacksmiths, or in other skilled trades.

The Money Changers

These restrictions pushed many Jews into becoming merchants and shopkeepers. Others became money changers. In those days Germany was not a country, but a collection of states, each with its own currency. Various currencies were also in use throughout the continent, particularly Eastern Europe. Many Jews had been pushed from place to place and so were knowledgeable about these currencies. The money changers provided non-Jewish businessmen and traders with advice about the value of the money used in other places, and also changed money for them for a small fee.

At this time, outlaws were common throughout Europe, and robberies of travelers were frequent. Some of the Jewish money changers had relatives and friends in other cities. When tradesmen wanted to avoid the risk of robbery, the money changer in one place would give them a note in Hebrew to a contact in another city. The note would identify them and state how much money was in their account. This was known as a letter of credit, valid only to the person to whom it was issued and useless to thieves.

Sometimes a trader would not have enough cash on hand to purchase the goods he was going to fetch. In such cases the Jewish money changer might lend him the money, charging a low rate of interest to be paid back when the goods were sold. In this way a small number of Jews became bankers. Some of them became wealthy. This small group would give rise to the myth of Jewish financial power in a world where most money and power would remain in non-Jewish hands.

Restrictions Eased; Prejudice Lingers

Jews were different from the general population of the countries in which they settled. They had different customs. They followed a different religion. They dressed differently, wearing skullcaps, prayer shawls, or other clothing associated with their faith. Because they were herded together in ghettoes, these differences were magnified. Anti-Semitism was widespread in Germany and Eastern Europe before the twentieth century.

However, when Germany became a nation in 1871, there was a lifting—in stages—of anti-Semitic laws. By 1900, Jews could own property, and while still subject to some minor restrictions, they were better off under German law than in most European countries. Many Jews stayed in the ghettoes because they hadn't enough money to leave. Those who could afford it—usually merchants or bankers—bought homes in middle-class neighborhoods and sent their children to private schools with German children. Many poor Germans, peasants and workers, resented this.

They complained that these Jews had succeeded only by lying, cheating, and stealing. They muttered that those Jews who stayed in the ghettoes remained only because it was their Jewish nature to live in filth while hoarding their gold. Legally, the Jews may now have been full German citizens, but there was still much prejudice against them.

Scapegoats of Defeat

In World War I, large numbers of Jews served in the German army. Many won medals, including the top honor of all, the Iron Cross. Following Germany's defeat in the war, however, Jews met with a resurgence of anti-Semitism.

During the winter of 1918–1919, there was a food shortage and "widespread starvation" in Germany.[6] Jews owned or ran many of the stores that sold food. Often their shelves were empty. When they weren't, the storekeepers were forced to pass along high prices charged by their suppliers. Many

Germans blamed the Jews for the shortage of food and accused them of getting rich from it.

Jews were also blamed for Germany losing the war. It was rumored that Jewish arms manufacturers had supplied inferior weapons at exorbitant prices, and that these had cost the lives of German soldiers. In addition, the accusation was made that high interest on government loans by Jewish bankers had robbed Germany of the money needed to win the war. Actually, it was non-Jewish firms (like the major German arms manufacturer, Krupps) that supplied arms to the German military, and the banks were mostly German owned. The few Jewish banks that loaned the government money did so at the same rate as all the other lending institutions.

Anti-Semitic Policy Evolves

Following the war, the Nazi party was born. It pledged to make Germany *Judenrein*. "Point Four of the Party program of February 24, 1920," read as follows: "Only a member of the [German] race can be a citizen. . . . no Jew can be a member of the race."[7]

Soon after Nazi party leader Adolf Hitler came to power in Germany in 1933, "Jews were denied the right to hold public office or civil service positions; they were excluded from farming; they were denied employment by press or radio." The following year "Jews were excluded from stock exchanges." In 1935 the Nuremberg Laws deprived Jews of their citizenship. They were forbidden to marry or to have other relationships with Germans or to employ German women or (even if they were war veterans) to display the German flag. In 1937 the death penalty was decreed for Jews who transferred their personal property from Germany to other countries. In 1938, "Jews were excluded from certain city areas, sidewalks, transportation, places of amusement, and restaurants; they were denied the right to practice law or medicine; they were excluded from business in general" and made to pay special taxes and fines. They had to register all property and could only sell it if they received official permission. In 1939 "they were excluded from the practice of dentistry" and ordered to turn over to the Nazis all jewelry and objects made of precious metals. In 1940 they were denied their right to payment by insurance companies for damage to their property in raids by Nazi thugs. In 1943 they were denied any rights in courts of law, "and the police were given complete discretion in imposing punishments, including even death."[8]

These anti-Jewish laws were backed up by acts of brutality. The most infamous of these was *Kristallnacht*—the Night of Broken Glass—on November 9–10, 1938. Some 7,500 Jewish shops and businesses were vandalized, their windows and doors smashed, 800 of them completely destroyed. Of the 191 synagogues razed, most were burned to the ground. Hundreds of Jewish homes were broken into, their furniture smashed, their valuables stolen. Some were torched and went up in flames. Some Jewish women were raped. More than ninety Jews were killed. Thirty thousand Jews—mostly men—were seized and shipped to concentration camps.

The First Mass Murders

Many more German Jews were eventually sent to extermination camps in the East and were killed there. The year after *Kristallnacht* the German army invaded Poland and World War II began. Now the Nazis expanded their deadly persecution of German Jews to include all the Jews of Europe. Now the entire continent was to be *Judenrein*.

In July 1941, Hitler's deputy, *Reichmarschall* Hermann Göring, issued the order for the "final solution of the Jewish question."[9] As the German army moved east through Poland and deep into Russia, Nazi killing squads followed. Jews were rounded up and shot, or put in ghettoes and killed later. In the conquered countries of Western Europe they were herded into boxcars and shipped to death camps.

Between the issuing of the Final Solution order in July 1941 and mid-March 1942, approximately one million Jews were murdered. In Eastern Europe they were at first the victims of SS units called *Einsatzgruppen*. The orders to these units were "that all Jews were supposed to be exterminated without regard to age or sex."[10] Later, thirty-eight battalions of Order Police were sent to help the *Einsatzgruppen*. These Order Police were civil servants and other civilians not considered fit for army duty. They were older men, often married with families. Most were not members of the Nazi party. Nevertheless, they shot Jews (including infants and children), and implemented the killings in the gas vans. Sometimes they were helped by Ukrainians, Latvians, and others.

Deniers in Denial

In mid-March 1942, acting on the recommendations of the Wannsee Conference held the previous January, efforts were stepped up to kill the Jews more quickly and efficiently. Industry, transportation networks, and army and police units in Germany and other countries joined forces to kill the millions of European Jews still alive. The result was the most enormous genocide in history.

The Holocaust deniers say the mass killings, the shootings and gassings, never happened. They say the extermination camps never existed. They say the Jews died of illness, as a natural result of wartime hardships, or of old age. They say that all evidence to the contrary is part of a plot hatched by international Jewry. They claim that the Holocaust is the greatest "hoax of the twentieth century."[11]

That's what they say—and more.

Hitler's defeat was the defeat of Europe. And of America. How could we have been so blind? The blame, it seems, must be laid at the door of the international Jews. It was their propaganda, lies, and demands that blinded the west to what Germany was doing.[1]

—Willis Carto, founder of
the Institute for Historical Review

olocaust deniers often call themselves "revisionists." They do this to make it seem as if they are merely reinterpreting the facts of history rather than rewriting and distorting them. Perhaps the best-known revisionist is British journalist and historian David Irving.

A "Moderate Fascist"

Irving has produced an impressive body of work. He has been writing books and articles dealing with the Nazis and World War II since the late 1960s. According to *The New York Times*: "Mr. Irving spent years poring over Nazi archives, rooting out long-lost diaries and private correspondence and presenting his findings in vivid, readable narratives that conveyed World War II from the German point of view."[2]

A "moderate fascist" is how David Irving defines himself.[3] In 1981 he founded a political party with the aim of assuming leadership of Great Britain. He keeps a portrait of Adolf Hitler over his desk, a token of his admiration for the Nazi dictator. In his book *Hitler's War*, Irving claimed that Hitler had no knowledge of the Final Solution or the Holocaust. This led renowned British historian Hugh Trevor-Roper to define Irving as a person who focuses on a small and doubtful shred of evidence and then uses it to dismiss any evidence that disproves his point. With this tactic, and with his use of half-truths, Irving is typical of other Holocaust deniers who lack his reputation.

In 1992, Irving said publicly that "there were no gas chambers at Auschwitz."[4] As a result, he was tried, convicted, and fined in a court in Germany, where Holocaust denial is a crime. In Great Britain, however, Holocaust denial is not a crime. That is where David Irving brought a libel suit against Professor Deborah Lipstadt because of what she wrote about him in her book *Denying the Holocaust: The Growing Assault on Truth and Memory.*

The Free-Speech Issue

At the time Professor Lipstadt's book came out, Irving had a contract with St. Martin's Press of New York to publish his biography *Goebbels, Mastermind of the Third Reich.* Following Professor Lipstadt's comments and other criticism of him as a Holocaust denier, St. Martin's canceled publication of the book. Irving then sued Professor Lipstadt for damages, claiming she had harmed his reputation as a writer and interfered with his ability to make a living. The trial attracted worldwide attention.

A libel charge is hard to defend under British law. The burden of proof is on the defendant to prove that what he or she wrote is true. Professor Lipstadt had written that Irving was "one of the most dangerous spokespersons for Holocaust denial," with a talent for distorting facts to fit his opinions. Irving accused her of being the tool of an "international endeavor" organized by Jewish world leaders to destroy his career.[5]

There was also the free-speech issue raised by the publisher's decision to cancel publication of Irving's biography of Goebbels. No other American publisher would agree to publish the book. Was Irving being muzzled because of his controversial opinions regarding the Holocaust?

The New York Times asked: "Can a writer who thinks the Holocaust was a hoax still be a great historian?" Raul Hilberg, author of the Holocaust classic *The Destruction of the European Jews,* defends Irving's right to publish his opinion that the Holocaust did not take place, but at the same time points out that this "is not a legitimate controversy." Historian Gordon Craig of Stanford University believes that "silencing Mr. Irving would be a high price to pay for freedom from the annoyance he causes us. The fact is that he knows more about National Socialism [Nazism] than most professional scholars in his field." On the other hand, History Professor Michael Geyer of the University of Chicago believes that Irving's bias is responsible for serious "flaws in his work."[6]

Among these flaws is Irving's insistence that Nazi evidence should be accepted and believed while the testimony of Holocaust survivors should be dismissed as worthless. "Eyewitness testimony," he has said of statements by survivors, "is really a matter for psychiatric evaluation."[7] British high court Justice Charles Gray, who presided over the libel case, found that such statements confirmed what Professor Lipstadt had written about Irving. Justice Gray declared that Irving "deliberately misrepresented and manipulated historical evidence." He found Irving to be an anti-Semite who "associates with right-wing extremists who promote neo-Nazism."[8] David Irving lost his libel suit against Professor Lipstadt.

Ernst Zundel's Trial

Although lacking David Irving's reputation as a World War II historian, Ernst Christhof Friedrich Zundel is also an influential Holocaust denier. Zundel was born in 1939 in the Black Forest area of Germany. When he was eighteen, he emigrated to Canada where he became a photo retoucher. He also became interested in neo-Nazi causes and was soon describing himself as a National Socialist (Nazi). He established a publishing house, Samisdat, which caters to rank-and-file neo-Nazis, race segregationists, members of the Ku Klux Klan, anti-Semites, and others whose causes are based on bigotry.

Zundel, along with George Dietz, is the coauthor of *The Hitler We Loved and Why,* a positive portrait and defense of the Führer (leader) of Nazi Germany, which absolves Hitler of any responsibility for the death of Jews in World War II.

The book was written under the pseudonym Friedrich Christhof, and established Zundel as a Holocaust revisionist. It was not as a writer, however, but rather as a publisher that Zundel attracted international attention. Nor was it a book that brought him wide notoriety. Rather, it was a thirty-two page pamphlet published by Zundel entitled *Did Six Million Really Die?*

The author of the pamphlet was an Englishman using the pen name Harwood. The pamphlet denied the reality of the Holocaust. Zundel was brought to trial in Toronto District Court under a law making it a crime to publish "a statement, tale or news that he knows is false and that causes, or is likely to cause, injury or mischief to a public interest." During the course of the trial Zundel told the court that he would not deny the "fundamental goodness of the Hitler party." He was found guilty and sentenced to nine months in jail.[9]

Since his release, Zundel has spoken at many neo-Nazi meetings and rallies, mainly in Europe. He claims that by speaking in opposition to the Holocaust myth he is striking a blow for freedom of speech. At the same time, Zundel has been active in distributing a pamphlet soliciting support for a worldwide campaign to ban Steven Spielberg's acclaimed film *Schindler's List*.

Hatemongers and Rabble-Rousers

Zundel, like the majority of Holocaust deniers both in the United States and abroad, falls into the category of hatemongers and rabble-rousers who don't concern themselves with truth. Rather, they steal a page from Hitler's book *Mein Kampf* (My Struggle), in which the Nazi dictator declared that the bigger and more outrageous the lie, the more likely it is to be believed by most people. The deniers' big lie is that the Holocaust never happened. They say it has been invented as part of a worldwide Jewish conspiracy.

Their tactics are often despicable. Genocide denier Ditlieb Felderer, for instance, mails strands of hair to European Jews—some of them Holocaust survivors—accompanied by notes asking them if they can prove the hair comes from a Jewish victim of the gas chambers. He has written articles relating sex to

Revisionist historian David Irving arrives at the High Court in London at the start of his libel trial.

the Holocaust, including one describing the effect of poison gas on women's sex organs. Felderer has been convicted and served time in jail in Sweden for distributing his hate literature.

American denier Jack Wikoff leads anti-African-American marches demanding "White Power." During these marches, and on other occasions, he hands out posters with cruelly exaggerated illustrations of Jews and African Americans with the caption *Where's Your Outrage, White America?* Wikoff calls Martin Luther King Jr.'s birthday the "Marchin' Lootin' Coon Holiday." Despite his bigotry, Wikoff is permitted to lecture to students at various colleges on Holocaust revisionism.

Greg Raven heads the Institute of Historical Review (IHR), an organization that claims to be motivated by a "deep dedication to the cause of truth in history."[10] (Its critics point out that it is actually driven by an anti-Jewish bias that distorts history.) Raven began his career writing material for stand-up comics and articles for automotive magazines. He claims the Holocaust never happened, but says he can't prove it because it isn't possible to prove a negative. Raven also says that Adolf Hitler was good for Germany, and that his greatness exceeded that of Franklin Roosevelt and Winston Churchill put together. Raven, like Felderer and Wikoff, frequently gives lectures on Holocaust denial to groups with racist and anti-Semitic agendas.

A Leading Anti-Semite

These men are followers of Willis Carto. He is "the most important and powerful anti-Semite in the United States,"[11] according to the Anti-Defamation League (ADL), which monitors bigotry in America. In 1979 he founded the Institute of Historical Research, presently headed by Greg Raven.

Willis Carto was in his late twenties in the 1950s when he joined the John Birch Society. The society was in favor of white supremacy, against civil rights for African Americans, anti-immigration, and anti-Semitic. However, it wasn't militant enough for Willis Carto. He wanted stronger measures to be taken against Jews. His extremism brought him into conflict with Robert Welch, the John Birch Society leader. Although Welch was himself an anti-Semite, he expelled Carto from the society.

In 1958, Carto organized the Liberty Lobby, defined by him as "a pressure group for patriotism."[12] Carto solicited contributions for the Liberty Lobby and subscriptions to its newspaper, *Spotlight.* By the 1980s contributions were coming in to Liberty Lobby at the rate of four million dollars a year. *Spotlight* had more than 330,000 subscribers.

Columnist Drew Pearson wrote that Liberty Lobby was "infiltrated by Nazis who revere the memory of Hitler," while conservative commentator William Buckley called the organization a "hotbed of anti-Semitism."[13] When *The Wall Street Journal* called Carto and the Liberty Lobby anti-Semitic in print, he sued the newspaper. He lost the case.

Carto then formed a publishing company, Noontide Press. In 1969, Noontide Press published *The Myth of the Six Million,* a 119-page book that "undertook to disprove all the evidence of the murder of the European Jews and to discredit all eyewitness testimony."[14] The author of the book was anonymous.

The Myth of the Six Million

An introduction to *The Myth of the Six Million* was written under an alias by Willis Carto himself. In it he explained that the reason the author had not used his name was that he "wished to protect his standing in the academic community by hiding his identity."[15] However, in 1969, David L. Hoggan claimed that he was the author and sued Noontide Press for money he said they owed him. Four years later he withdrew the suit, possibly after a settlement was reached with Carto. A new edition of *The Myth,* brought out by Noontide in 1974, was still authored by Anonymous. To this day, *The Myth of the Six Million* remains a source of material for Holocaust deniers.

In Surrey, England, a pamphlet based on *The Myth* was published by Historical Review Press. It was promoted as a work of history by "a specialist in political and diplomatic aspects of the Second World War," claiming to be a University of London scholar.[16] Actually, the author was the editor of a magazine published by the National Front, a British neo-Nazi organization.

Implying that works on Holocaust denial were connected to educational institutions was an attempt to give them a respectability they lacked. It was what Carto had tried to do when he suggested that the anonymous author of *The Myth of the Six Million* was a distinguished educator. It was what led him to found the Institute of Historical Review. It was the reason the IHR contrived to hold its first so-called Revisionist Convention on the Los Angeles Northrup College campus in 1979.

The Hoax of the Twentieth Century

In 1980 the IHR began publishing the quarterly *Journal of Historical Review*. The lead article in the first issue was by A. R. Butz, a professor at Northwestern University. Four years earlier Butz had written *The Hoax of the Twentieth Century*, which denied the Holocaust. The book had been published by Historical Review Press in Surrey, England—the company that fronted for the neo-Nazi National Front. It was later brought out in the United States by Carto's Noontide Press.

Although a university professor, Butz was no expert when it came to the Holocaust. His field is electrical engineering. When this was pointed out, Butz responded that professional historians have been frightened away from questioning a subject as widely accepted as the Nazi genocide of the Jews. Therefore, he reasoned, it is up to scholars like himself to expose what he calls the "propaganda hoax."[17]

The Hoax of the Twentieth Century is supported by scholarly footnotes, quotes from Holocaust works by prominent historians, and references to legitimate research centers and archives. Given such reputable sources, *The Hoax of the Twentieth Century* should present a carefully reasoned point of view. However, the book is not only poorly written and badly organized, it is also illogical and inconsistent.

Butz had been critical of *The Myth of the Six Million* for containing errors of fact. At the same time, he praised the revisionist work of French geographer Paul Rassinier for concluding that the extermination of the Jews was "a historic lie."[18] According to Butz, the purpose of this lie is to further the goals of the State of Israel. It is successful, he says, because Jews are among "the most powerful groups on earth."[19]

That Jews are so powerful was, of course, the view of the original Nazis. Claiming Jews invented the Holocaust not only denies their suffering, it also confirms the myth that Jews have a plan to manipulate the world in order to dominate it. This is a key element of both Holocaust denial and anti-Semitism generally.

To persecute a group, the group must first be labeled inferior and then escalated into a fearsome threat. To do this, both truth and reality must be ignored. When that happens, a very real threat arises. It is the threat of another Holocaust.

I told them that, if they [Jews] precipitated another war, they would not be spared and that I would exterminate the vermin throughout Europe, once and for all . . . . Well, we have lanced the Jewish abscess; and the world of the future will be eternally grateful to us.[1]

—Adolf Hitler gloating in his bunker
shortly before his suicide in 1945

German dictator Adolf Hitler lives in the minds of many Holocaust deniers as a martyr to racial superiority. He was, they imply—and sometimes say outright—the victim of a worldwide Jewish conspiracy. While they claim that the Holocaust never happened, they are quick to add that in any case Hitler had nothing to do with it. If some individuals were so outraged by Jewish treachery that they took action against Jews, such isolated cases could hardly be blamed on Hitler. Indeed, *Nation Europa*, a prominent German neo-Nazi journal, insists that there is no "evidence that Hitler knew of the mad doings of a small clique of criminals."[2]

The Genocide Promise

Holocaust revisionists do not deny that Hitler was an anti-Semite. In his autobiography, *Mein Kampf,* published in 1925 before the Nazis came to power, he wrote of "the nightmare vision of the seduction of hundreds of thousands of girls by repulsive crooked-legged Jew bastards."[3] This is only one of the fantasies by which Hitler demonized Jews.

On January 30, 1933, Hitler became chancellor of Germany. On March 23 the Reichstag (the German parliament) passed the Enabling Act, which in effect made Hitler dictator of Germany with absolute power. On April 1, 1933, government billboards went up all over Germany. "Do not buy from Jews!" was the message.[4] It was backed up by anti-Semitic speeches by Hitler's recently appointed Minister of Propaganda Joseph Goebbels. There followed the series of laws, all approved by Hitler, which deprived German Jews, and then other European Jews, of their property, rights, freedom, and finally their lives.

Hitler's defenders claim that when he and other high-ranking Nazis discussed the "final solution of the Jewish question, they were talking about Jewish emigration to Palestine, or the Russian interior, or other non-Nazi countries."[5] However, shortly before World War II began, in a speech to the Reichstag, Hitler promised that the upcoming war would bring about "the destruction of the Jewish race in Europe."[6] He referred to this promise in six major speeches delivered after the war began.

What Hitler Knew

Regarding Hitler's responsibility for, and even knowledge of, the genocide of the Jews, David Irving insists that "the kind of evidence against Hitler" does not bear scrutiny.[7] Unbiased historians, however, find it overwhelming. It speaks for itself, as follows:

A 1941 memorandum from Germany's governor-general of Poland, Dr. Hans Frank, to German Secretary of State Dr. Joseph Buhler informs him that "Europe's Jews were to be liquidated on Adolf Hitler's orders."[8] A 1942 directive from *Reichsführer* Heinrich Himmler to the concentration camp commandants he supervised reminded them that "it is the Führer's wish to have the Jews disappear from the face of the earth."[9] Later Himmler reported to Hitler that between August 1942 and the end of November 1942, 363,211 Jews had been executed. On February 24, 1943, Hitler assured a Sports Palace audience that the war would end "with the extermination of the Jewish people in Europe."[10]

Further evidence of Hitler's involvement was provided by top Nazis during their postwar trials for crimes against humanity. Adolf Eichmann, in charge of transporting Jews to the extermination camps, testified that in August 1941, Gestapo (Nazi secret police) chief Reinhard Heydrich told him that "the fuhrer has ordered the physical extermination of the Jews."[11] *Reichskommissar* Erich Koch, who had been in charge of killing 500,000 to 600,000 Jews in the Ukraine, swore that he had acted "under personal verbal orders from Hitler."[12]

Neither this testimony nor a wealth of other evidence convinces the neo-Nazi National Socialist White American Party that Hitler was involved in the Holocaust. They say that "once this great and colossal LIE has been vanquished for all time, then White People, all over the world, will be able to see Adolf Hitler as the great leader of the White race and the greatest hero of the 20th century."[13] Their logic is that Hitler couldn't have been involved because the Holocaust never happened anyway.

The Protocols

The deniers view the Holocaust as a Jewish Communist plot financed by Jewish international bankers. They say the plot is designed to convince a gullible public of horrifying propaganda distributed by the Jewish-controlled world media. One of the purposes behind this scheme, in their view, is to obtain reparations for the Jews from the German nation, as well as other countries that collaborated with the Nazis. Another purpose, they say, is to tighten the control of the worldwide Jewish conspiracy over the Christian peoples of the world.

This conspiracy theory is based on a vicious anti-Semitic book called *The Protocols of the Learned Elders of Zion*, which was published in Russia in 1903. In it, forged documents were used to expose a Jewish plot to conquer the world and enslave Christians. At that time there was fear of a revolution by the peasants against the wealthy aristocratic landowners of Russia. *The Protocols* were written and circulated with the specific intent of diverting peasant anger away from the landowners and directing it toward the Jews. Today, updated new editions of *The Protocols* are being printed in many languages and are on sale in the United States, Europe, South America, and Japan. These are still quoted by anti-Semites and Holocaust deniers to justify their bigotry.

Like many conspiracy theories, this one has elements of paranoia. One definition of paranoia defines it as a mental disorder, which distorts reality and raises fear of people different from oneself. Paranoia also requires that one build up arguments to support the fear, and to justify the actions taken against those who are the object of it. These elements were already present in the Nazi movement as it moved toward taking over Germany in the 1920s and 1930s.

Whitewashing the Camps

Nazi persecution of German Jews had attracted worldwide attention by 1933. To protest it, Jews in other countries organized a boycott of German products. The Nazis immediately accused international Jewry of declaring war against Germany. The deniers say this justified putting the German Jews in concentration camps. After World War II actually began, they say that the Jews in countries conquered by the Nazis were rounded up and put in camps because they were organized to sabotage the German war effort. They insist that the Germans had every right to lock up Jewish civilians between 1933 and 1945. They say the Jews were prisoners of war (POWs).

Jews were not, however, treated as prisoners of war. They were used as slave labor, starved, and worked to death. Millions were simply slaughtered in violation of international law.

Not so, say the deniers. Jews were much too valuable a workforce to be starved or executed. They do not, however, comment on the children who were too young to work, nor on those too sick or old to work. Camp records show that the young, the old, and the infirm were killed immediately upon their arrival at Auschwitz, Treblinka, and other extermination camps.

Facts and Fantasy

Arguments denying the Holocaust start with truth and then twist it to suit the purpose of the deniers. The truth is that typhus and other diseases were widespread during the war. The movements of troops and prisoners, POWs and Jews in boxcars, fleeing refugees and forest animals on the run from cannon fire—all these generated unsanitary conditions. Lice thrive in such conditions, and lice carry disease. Many of those in the concentration camps died of these diseases. The deniers insist that this was "the main reason for a high death rate in the camps."[14] They say that during the closing days of the war there was both a shortage of medical supplies and general chaos, and that this was the cause of large numbers of Jewish deaths.

They deny that there was any deliberate policy to exterminate Jews. They even have an explanation for the million Jews murdered by special killing squads in Eastern Europe before the extermination camps were put into operation: They say it never happened. Seizing on the fact that many Polish Jews fled to Russia to escape the German army, they claim that "the Soviets deported virtually all of the Jews of eastern Poland to their interior in 1940."[15] At the end of the war, they say, these Jews fled west and eventually ended up in what is now Israel, or in the United States. They claim that many went to New York City, "the home of millions of Jews," where, unnoticed, they merged with the Jews already there.[16]

Such statements may have small kernels of truth. Despite strict immigration quotas, some Jewish Holocaust survivors did go to New York and settle there. Some Polish Jews fled east, then west, and then got out of Europe. However, it is Nazi records that confirm the deaths in the gas chambers and the murder of one million Polish Jews by killing squads. The deniers' theory is just that—a theory—with no hard evidence to support it.

The Diary of Anne Frank

This is also true of revisionist attacks on what is perhaps the most widely read document to come out of World War II, *The Diary of Anne Frank*. A journal kept by a young Jewish girl who hid from the Nazis in an Amsterdam attic, Anne Frank's day-to-day record of her life has touched the hearts of people

Pages from Anne Frank's diary were placed under scrutiny in 1981 in an effort to prove that the writings were authentic.

around the world. It has sold more than 20 million copies in forty countries. According to the deniers, however, "the famous diary is a literary hoax."[17]

The facts are as follows: On July 5, 1942, when Anne Frank was thirteen years old, in order to escape the roundups of Jews by Nazis, the entire Frank family went into hiding. They shared their small attic hiding place for two years with the Van Daan family, including their fifteen-year-old son, Peter, and an elderly Jewish dentist—eight people in all. During those two years, Anne never left the attic.

Her diary is an account of her life there. It details the daily frictions among the eight people in the attic. It describes the attraction between her and Peter Van Daan. It talks about the difficulties of smuggling in enough food to feed everyone. She writes of listening with pounding heart as the Gestapo searched the area just beyond their secret hiding place.

On August 4, 1944, the Gestapo learned of the hiding place from an informant and arrested all those in the attic. Anne was separated from her parents and sent to Auschwitz in Poland. Auschwitz was a death camp, but Anne was young and healthy and able to work, so she was not killed. In October 1944, Anne was shipped to the Belsen camp in Germany. A typhus epidemic had broken out there. In March 1945, fifteen-year-old Anne died of the disease.

Denying the Deniers

The Diary of Anne Frank became a major target for Holocaust deniers because of its popularity with teen readers, who were moved by her story. In many ways they could identify with Anne. If the deniers could convince young people that the book was a fraud, that would raise doubts in their minds as to the authenticity of the Holocaust itself. It provided an ideal target for those rewriting history with the goal of influencing future generations.

Anne had written in her diary of a vacuum cleaner being used. The deniers jumped on this detail and asked how people in hiding could have used such a noisy appliance without being detected. They ignored the fact that the attic hiding place was in a warehouse and that Anne had specifically written that the workers had gone home and the building—except for the attic—was empty before the vacuum was used.

Because Anne had described her sexual feelings toward Peter, deniers attacked the book as child pornography. At the same time that they denied Anne's authorship, they called her a sex fiend. They added that the obsession with sex was well known to be a trait peculiar to Jews. They ignored the fact that all young people have such feelings, and that Anne's honesty in relating them is one of the reasons teens relate so well to her diary.

Another accusation was that the diary had been written with a ballpoint pen. Deniers pointed out that such pens weren't in use in Amsterdam in the 1940s. They also charged that the paper on which Anne's diary had been written was not produced until the 1950s.

This charge was serious enough to be considered by the Netherlands State Institute for War Documentation in 1981. The institute had Anne Frank's handwritten diaries examined by the Dutch State Forensic Science Laboratory of the Ministry of Justice. The laboratory conducted extensive examinations and tests of the diary's ink and paper and issued a 270-page report. The document summed up the evidence confirming that the diary was genuine and that it had indeed been written by Anne Frank when she was between thirteen and fifteen years old. No ballpoint pen had been used by Anne. The report specifically shot down the deniers' charge that the diary was a forgery.

Despite conclusive evidence disproving them, the deniers still continue to repeat their charges against *The Diary of Anne Frank*. Perhaps it is because its message is so completely opposed to their cause. "If God lets me live," Anne had written in her diary, ". . . I shall work in the world and for mankind!"[18] The deniers, however, have a different goal. Like the original Nazis, they work to establish neo-Nazi superiority over the people of the world.

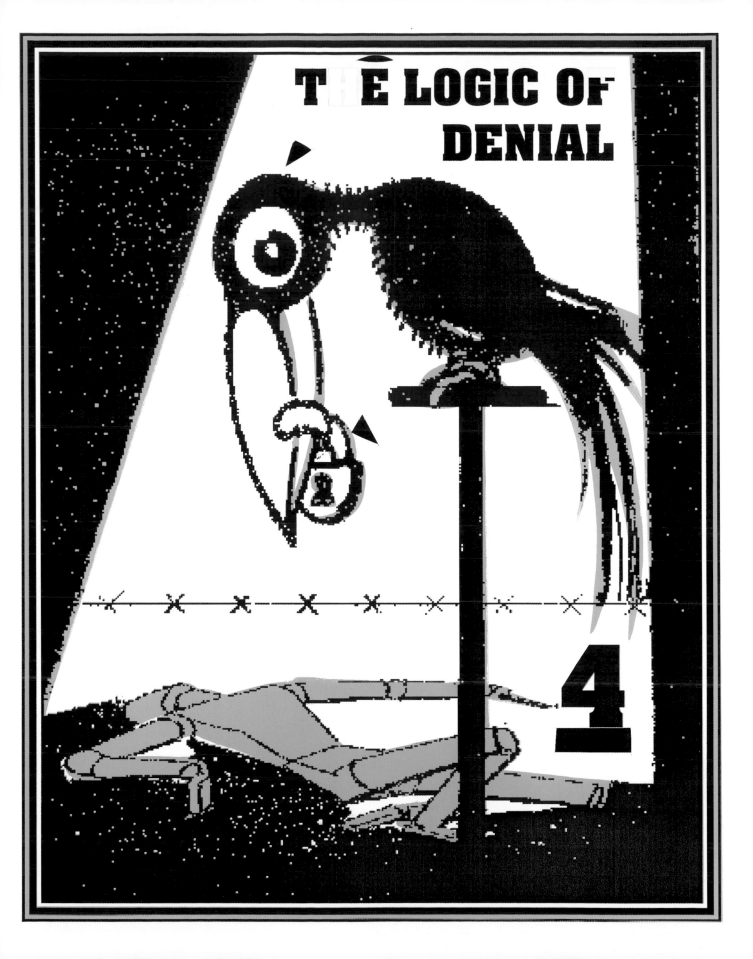

The Hitler gas chambers never existed. The gassing installations found in Auschwitz were really crematoria for cremating corpses of those who had died from a variety of causes, including the "genocidic" Anglo-American bombing raids.[1]

—From a pamphlet by Holocaust denier Austin J. App

Austin App began denying that the Holocaust had occurred soon after the end of World War II. He was neither a journalist nor a historian, but rather a professor of English at the University of Scranton and LaSalle College in Pennsylvania. His argument was that the Jews had pulled off a colossal deception. The purpose of the deception, he said, was to demonize Germany in the eyes of the world. The goal was to create sympathy for Jews in order to finance a Jewish state.

The Hoess Testimony

The Holocaust had, of course, created sympathy for the Jews. That sympathy had helped finance the creation of the Jewish State of Israel. However, these consequences in no way cancel out the overwhelming proof that approximately three million of the six million Jews who died in the Holocaust died in the gas chambers of camps such as Auschwitz. Among the volumes of documentation is this testimony by Auschwitz camp commandant Rudolf Hoess:

"[We] used Zyklon B which was a crystalized prussic acid which we dropped into the death chamber from a small opening. It took from three to fifteen minutes to kill the people in the death chamber depending upon climatic conditions. We knew when the people were dead because their screaming stopped. . . . After the bodies were removed our special Kommandos took off the

Rudolf Hoess, former commandant of Auschwitz, on trial in Poland

rings and extracted the gold from the teeth of the corpses. . . . Children of tender years were invariably exterminated since by reason of their youth they were unable to work."[2]

According to Holocaust denier Mark Weber, "the postwar 'confession' of Auschwitz commandant Rudolf Hoess, which is a crucial part of the Holocaust extermination story, is a false statement that was obtained by torture."[3] Further doubt has been cast on Hoess's testimony, and on other accounts of the gas chamber killings, by the Institute for Historical Review. The IHR says that "torture was extensively used to produce fraudulent 'evidence' for the infamous Nuremberg trials, and in other postwar 'war crimes' trials."[4]

The torturers, according to some deniers, were Jews disguised in British uniforms. They say that hundreds of key Nazis were tortured into confessing to crimes that they never committed, or into framing their fellow Nazis for those crimes in the war crimes trials, which took place between late 1945 and the 1960s. Many of these trials were held in German courts. Holocaust deniers' claim that this was because the Jews had secretly infiltrated the postwar German government in order to condemn the German people in the eyes of the world.

Such infiltration, they say, was part of a secret conspiracy of Jews, which started around 1941. That was the beginning, say the deniers, of a campaign to forge documents to prove that a Holocaust had taken place. Allegedly, hundreds of such documents were planted in Nazi files by Jewish conspirators. The deniers conclude with the charge that after the war the Jews rounded up all the camp survivors and told them what to say to prove that the Nazis had used poison gas to exterminate the Jews.

Denying the Evidence

Disproving the mass killings of Jews in gas chambers is key to establishing that there has been no genocide. That is why the deniers emphasize that documents proving their existence are forgeries. Among those put into evidence at the Nazi war crimes trials was a letter of acceptance from the company that was awarded the contract to build the ovens for burning the bodies at Auschwitz, I. A. Topf and Sons of Erfurt, Germany. The letter acknowledges receipt of an order "for five triple furnaces, including two electric elevators for raising the corpses and one emergency elevator." The Didier Works of Berlin, in its bid to supply furnaces to a camp at Belgrade, suggested that "each furnace . . . have an oven measuring only 24 by 18 inches, as coffins will not be used."[5] There are bills from Tesch and Stabenow of Hamburg for two tons of Zyklon-B crystals a month to be used at Auschwitz. There are also written orders from Tesch and Stabenow offering to supply ventilation equipment for extermination chambers. (The firm's partners were hanged as war criminals in 1946.) The Desau firm of Degesch billed for three quarters of a ton of cyanide crystals a month. Countless documents implicating German firms like I. G. Farben and Krupp confirm the genocide. They are all forgeries, according to the Holocaust deniers.

When the concentration camps were liberated, photographers and movie cameramen took pictures of heaps of hundreds of skeletal dead bodies. Some Holocaust revisionists say these pictures were faked. Other say that "piles of emaciated corpses do not mean that these people were 'gassed' or deliberately starved to death. Actually, these were tragic victims of raging epidemics or of starvation due to a lack of food in the camps toward the end of the war."[6] They claim that deliberately misleading captions were used with still photos, and deceitful voice-over narrations with motion-picture documentaries, in order to make people believe that genocide had taken place. However, they offer no evidence to prove that such deceptions occurred.

The Mermelstein Case

In addition to disproving the existence of the gas chambers and ovens, another major goal of the Institute for Historical Review has always been to get publicity. In 1979 the IHR offered to pay $50,000 to any person who "could prove that the Nazis operated gas-chambers to exterminate Jews during World War II."[7] When the offer didn't get the anticipated media attention, the IHR sent letters to prominent Holocaust survivors daring them to accept the challenge. Among those who received such letters was Mel Mermelstein, a survivor of Auschwitz who had attacked the IHR in various newspapers. Mermelstein's mother and sisters had been killed in the gas chambers at Auschwitz, and his father and brother had also been murdered by the Nazis. Eager to expose the IHR's anti-Semitic bigotry and to discredit the organization, Mermelstein took up the challenge.

He provided a notarized description of his imprisonment at Auschwitz, and of his observations of the gassing. He supplied other eyewitness testimony of the process by which victims were selected, the exterminations, and the ovens. He furnished scientific evidence and expert witnesses.

When the IHR did not respond to his claim, Mermelstein filed a lawsuit against them. The IHR contrived many lengthy delays of the case. Finally it was heard by Judge Thomas T. Johnson, who decided that it was a "fact that Jews were gassed to death at the Auschwitz Concentration Camp in Poland during the summer of 1944."[8] Mermelstein was awarded the $50,000 plus another $40,000 for pain and suffering. The IHR was ordered to provide a letter of apology to Mermelstein for the emotional harm their statements had caused him and others who had survived the gas chambers of Auschwitz.

On August 7, 1985, Mermelstein stated during a radio interview that the IHR had signed a judicial notice confirming the existence of gas chambers at Auschwitz. A year later the IHR sued him for libeling them on the radio program. Another year and a half passed, and then the IHR dropped the suit. Mermelstein then sued the IHR on the grounds that their suit had been ungrounded and malicious. That suit was later settled, but the terms of the settlement have not been revealed.

The "Execution Technologist"

The publicity generated by the Mermelstein case may well have made the cost worthwhile to the IHR. Their purpose was—and is—to make it appear that the argument as to the existence of the gas chambers in the Nazi extermination camps is a valid one. However, that validity was destroyed by circumstances that created even more attention. They involved a man named Fred A. Leuchter.

An "execution technologist"—this is how Fred Leuchter defines himself. He declares that he has been fascinated with death since he was a child. As an adult, Leuchter embarked on a career designing electric chairs for executing convicted criminals in death penalty cases. He went on to design a lethal injection machine for the state of New Jersey. "People executed by my machines have dignified, painless deaths," he boasts. "I sleep well at night."[9]

During the 1988 trial of Ernst Zundel, supporters of the Holocaust denier contacted Fred Leuchter to help with the defense. He was paid $35,000 to go to Poland and tour the former extermination camps of Auschwitz and Majdanek. The object was to help Zundel prove that the gas chambers were a myth. Leuchter had just recently been married. He and his bride, a photographer, spent their honeymoon in the former death camps collecting what Leuchter would insist was proof that there had been no gassing of inmates.

Rejected Expertise

The result of Leuchter's efforts was *The Leuchter Report: An Engineering Report on the Alleged Execution Gas Chambers at Auschwitz, Birkenau and Majdanek Poland*. *The Leuchter Report* was subsequently published by Samisdat (Zundel's company) and by Focal Point Publications (David Irving's publishing company) in London. Based on what Leuchter boasted was his expert knowledge, *The Leuchter Report* concluded that there had never been any deaths by gassing at the three camps.

When Leuchter took the stand to testify as an expert witness in the Zundel case, the prosecutor questioned his self-proclaimed expertise. Leuchter had to admit that he was not an engineer, had never studied advanced physics, and had no knowledge of toxicology (the study of poisons, their detection, and their effects). Presiding Judge Ronald Thomas concluded that Leuchter "has no expertise in this area."[10] He ruled that Leuchter had no standing as an expert witness when it came to the design and operation of gas chambers.

On the stand and in his report Leuchter claimed that he had obtained maps and blueprints of the gas chambers and crematoria from the camps' official archives. Officials at the former camps denied that he had ever received any such documents. He said that he had consulted with experts of the Du Pont chemical company regarding the substances used in the gas chambers. Du Pont denied this. He claimed to have consulted with the warden of California's San Quentin Prison about executions in its gas chambers. The warden denied having had any such consultation with Leuchter. A similar denial was made by the Department of Correction in North Carolina regarding Leuchter's testimony that they had consulted with him regarding the functioning of their execution gas chambers. In all, spokespersons for six states that performed executions by gas chambers contradicted Leuchter's claims to have advised them on the technology employed.

The Leuchter Report

The Leuchter Report is a highly technical document based on questionable evidence and incompetent interpretation. Its author lacks both the education and training to deal with its subject matter. Some of the claims made in *The Leuchter Report,* and the facts disproving them, are as follows:

The report claims to "scientifically demonstrate" that Zyklon-B did not kill people at Auschwitz. Zyklon-B is a powerful insecticide. Its crystals release hydrocyanic acid (HCN), a poisonous gas. According to Leuchter, the "technical difficulties" in releasing HCN to execute people could not have been overcome by the Nazis in the 1940s. The implication is that the expertise to do so had not yet been developed. In point of fact, the substance had been used in gas chambers in the United States as early as the 1920s. The Germans used it for delousing, and were quite aware of how to overcome any "technical difficulties."[11]

A further claim was that since more traces of HCN were found in the Auschwitz delousing chambers than in the "so-called extermination chambers," no Zyklon-B killings could have taken place in the latter.[12] The question is how Leuchter could have determined this since while the delousing chambers where he took samples were still intact, the extermination chambers had long since been destroyed. Furthermore, the concentration of HCN needed to kill lice must be fifty-three times as strong as that used to kill warm-blooded human beings. The process of delousing clothes took seventy-two hours. Gassing groups of people took fifteen to thirty minutes. Even if the extermination chambers had still been standing, because of the differences in concentration and time, they would not have showed traces of HCN to the extent that the delousing chambers did.

Scattered to the Winds

The Nazis would not have used Zyklon-B to kill people, according to Leuchter, because it is highly explosive, and, with the furnaces used to dispose of corpses so nearby, the risk would have been too great. However, the concentration of HCN necessary to cause an explosion would have had to be two hundred times greater than the mixture released in the gas chambers. *The Leuchter Report* also suggested that if Zyklon-B had been used, "the people who dropped the Zyklon-B into the chambers would have died from the gas themselves."[13] In fact, those who carried out the killings wore gas masks to prevent this from happening.[14] The report adds that "if the gas chambers were ventilated, the gas would kill the people outside."[15] This doesn't happen because once released into the open air, the concentration of HCN drops and it dissipates quickly. (Gas chambers in U. S. prisons are also ventilated this way.)[16] Leuchter claims it would have taken roughly twenty hours before a chamber could be safely entered following a gassing, adding that this disproves eyewitness accounts of bodies being removed within twenty to thirty minutes. This ignores the fact that the chambers were forcibly ventilated (meaning that the gas was pumped out through the ducts to dissipate in the open air). In some cases where victims were backed up waiting for the chambers to be used again, the *Sonderkommandos* (prisoners assigned to the grisly task of removing the bodies) wore gas masks.[17]

"The extermination chambers were actually morgues," according to *The Leuchter Report*. "Zyklon-B was used in them as a disinfectant." As a matter of scientific fact, "Zyklon-B is useless for disinfecting corpses, as it does not kill anaerobic bacteria"—the type of bacteria found in dead tissue.[18]

Leuchter claimed that the doors of the chambers used for extermination were too weak to withstand the pressure of people trying to escape. He offered photographs in support of this theory. However, they were pictures of the unfortified doors to the delousing chambers, not the doors reinforced with iron bars, which sealed victims inside the gas chambers.[19]

"If so many people were actually killed and cremated," asks *The Leuchter Report,* "where is all the ash?"[20] The answer is that when a body is cremated, the amount of ash remaining is little enough to fit in a small box. The ashes of thousands of people can fit into one fair-sized truck. Survivor testimony is that the ash was sometimes scattered over fields, sometimes buried, and sometimes (as at Auschwitz) dumped into a river.[21]

Disproving the scientific basis of *The Leuchter Report* denies the deniers any basis for their claim that the gassings did not happen. This punctures a major hole in their theories of Holocaust revisionism generally. It pushes them into proclaiming the twisted logic known as moral relativism.

Immediately after Japan declared war on the United States of America, the order was issued to round up all Americans of Japanese ancestry and imprison them in large camps. . . . The Germans . . . never implemented measures against the Jews as drastic as the United States did with their Japanese citizens . . . .[1]

—Anonymous Holocaust denial on the Internet

oral relativism is the technique used by deniers to make the Holocaust seem less horrible than it actually was by comparing it to other events. Usually, but not always, these other events are lesser evils. Generally, they are exaggerated. Always, the point is to make the evil of the Holocaust seem less by making other evils seem greater.

By this reasoning, the deniers justify genocide on the grounds that it has taken place before and will again. In times of war, they say, slaughter is the norm; there are civilian casualties; women and children die. If some Nazis did indeed commit crimes against humanity so, too, have others. Do the victors really have the right, the deniers ask, to judge the crimes of war?

This argument is used to justify the mass murder of helpless civilians. It removes responsibility from individuals, groups, and nations for such actions. If we are all guilty, it says, then no one is guilty; no one is responsible for genocide. The danger of such an argument is that it opens the way to another Holocaust.

The British Prison Ships

Half-truths are the hallmark of the moral relativism arguments made by Holocaust deniers. They begin, with some justification, by disputing that concentration camps were a German phenomenon. According to the Institute for Historical Review, concentration camps originated during the American

Revolution when the British interned colonists, thousands of whom died from whippings, beatings, and disease.

The facts are not in dispute. Their interpretation, however, is. Also, one small discrepancy leads to a larger one. American prisoners during the Revolutionary War were mostly housed on British prison ships, not in camps. A concentration camp, by definition, is an "internment center for political prisoners and members of national or minority groups who are confined for reasons of state security, exploitation or punishment."[2] British prison ships during the American Revolution were indeed filthy and inhumane places of confinement. However, they were prisoner-of-war (POW) installations, not concentration camps.

More than 11,000 American patriots died on the prison ships. They were soldiers, sailors, and others who had fought against the British. They were not civilians. They were not helpless children, women, or old people. The treatment of the American prisoners was horrendous, but they were not executed by the millions because of their ethnic identity or religion. The prison ships of the British during the American Revolution, as awful as they were, are a far cry from the Nazi extermination camps of the Holocaust.

Nor, as bad as it was, can the British treatment of POWs during the American Revolution be compared to the Nazi treatment of Russian POWs during World War II. Nazi records show that a large number of the 3.8 million Russian soldiers taken prisoner between June 21 and December 6, 1941, were deliberately starved and left outdoors in subzero cold to die. Nazi Minister for the Occupied Eastern Territories Alfred Rosenberg reported that "a large part of them have starved or died . . ." although "there was food enough in Russia to provide for them." He commented that "the more of these prisoners who die, the better it is for us."[3]

Boer War Concentration Camps

Revisionists and deniers, while failing in any sense to justify the Nazi death camps, are more accurate in their portrayal of the first concentration camps set up by Great

Britain during the Boer War. The Boers were descendants of Dutch and Huguenot settlers in South Africa. The territory was rich in gold and diamonds, and toward the end of the nineteenth century this encouraged many British to emigrate there. Soon there were conflicts between them and the Boers. In 1899, Great Britain sent a military force to come to the aid of British subjects in South Africa.

The Boers were tough guerrilla fighters, and for three years they thwarted the British army at every turn. Finally the British commander Lord Kitchener decided to "sweep the country clean of Boers. His troops moved into Boer settlements and herded all residents, including women and children, into concentration camps. Thousands of family members were locked up, and reports indicated large numbers of women and children died from starvation."[4]

Holocaust deniers eagerly compare this dreadful historical fact to the fate of the Jews in the Nazi extermination camps. They claim that "approximately 30,000 died in these (British) hell-holes, which were as terrible as German concentration camps of World War II."[5] Such comparisons are moral relativism at its most dangerous. Barbaric as they were, the approximately 30,000 British concentration camp deaths of 1902 cannot compare with the millions who died at the hands of the Nazis in the 1940s.

The Holocaust cannot be justified by pointing to other atrocities. It may be true that many nations and many groups have committed barbarous acts. But we do not find a person not guilty of murder because others have murdered before him. There are laws for nations as well as for people, and we dare not ignore them because they have been broken with impunity before.

The Internment of Japanese Americans

All injustices are equal in the eyes of the deniers. It follows that they equate the internment of Japanese Americans during World War II with the herding of Jews into concentration camps. They use a disgraceful action on the part of United States wartime authorities to excuse the state-authorized murder of millions of innocent people by the Nazis.

What happened was that the surprise Japanese attack on Pearl Harbor which propelled the United States into World War II prompted paranoid suspicions toward Japanese-American citizens as well as Japanese aliens. Regarded as potential spies, most Japanese Americans lived on the West Coast where there was a very real fear of a follow-up invasion by Japan. The federal government, although lacking any evidence of disloyalty, ordered the roundup of more than 100,000 Japanese-American men, women, and children. During this roundup, many of the Japanese Americans were deprived of their property, and some families were separated. The victims were shipped to internment camps in the interior of the country and kept there for as long as four or five years.

Holocaust deniers ask how Nazi concentration camps differed from these American "relocation" camps, claiming that "whereas the Germans interned persons on the basis of being real or suspected security threats to the war effort, the [President Franklin D.] Roosevelt administration interned persons on the basis of ethnicity alone." Their argument is that millions of Jews were not put in camps "on the basis of ethnicity" (because they were Jews), but rather because they were "a threat to national security." The deniers add that "Jews were overwhelmingly represented in Communist subversion." This ignores the original Nazi charge of a plot hatched by wealthy international Jewish bankers—surely no allies of communism. It dismisses the fact that most European Jews, particularly in Germany, were middle-class tradespeople and shopkeepers who were neither bankers, nor particularly sympathetic to left-wing causes.[6]

"A Bold-Faced Lie"

The Holocaust revisionist version of what happened to the Jews in Germany is an incredible anti-Semitic rewriting of history. They say that "the few Jews who were put into camps, after the election of Hitler as *Reichskanzler* (Chancellor of Germany) were those who employed harsh measures against the upcoming young Nazi-movement before the elections. Cruel judges, pornographers, communist leaders, open homosexuals, government criminals, financial con-artists, international speculators . . . they all got their 'day in court' and ended up in concentration camps. However, many of them were released after a short investigation, or after serving some time. But no one was put into a camp without a reason. As a matter of fact, thousands of Jews were not bothered by the Nazis or by the fate of their 'convicted' co-religionists. They went on with their daily lives in Germany while the world was running amok about the 'harsh treatment of Jews in Germany.' "[7]

The actual facts are these: When the Nazis took power in 1933, there were half a million Jews—about 1 percent of the population—in Germany. By 1939, when the war started, more than half the German Jews had fled the country. Of the roughly 240,000 who were left, 210,000—90 percent—were annihilated. To put it another way, German Jews who had been arrested and put in concentration camps were rarely, if ever, released. They were there not because they had committed any crime, but because they were Jewish, and that's why they were put to death. Only a handful of Jews managed to hide out in Germany, living "their daily lives," which meant managing to stay alive until the Nazis were defeated.[8]

By contrast, however wrong and unconstitutional the United States internment of Japanese Americans was, they were not murdered. They were deprived of their freedom, but they were not starved to death. While cruel medical experiments amounting to torture were performed on inmates of Nazi concentration camps—including children—no such operations occurred in the facilities used to house Japanese Americans. This comparison by the Holocaust deniers is best summed up by internationally esteemed French historian Pierre Vidal-Naquet, who writes that "it is a bold-faced lie to compare the Hitlerian camps to the camps set up, in a perfectly scandalous decision, by the Roosevelt administration to house Americans of Japanese origin."[9]

The Comparison to Slavery

There was an undeniably racist element to the internment of Japanese Americans during World War II. Holocaust revisionists are quick to point this out. In similar fashion they assert that the Nazis' treatment of the Jews was not as bad as the United States' treatment of black Americans has been. They point to slavery, an undeniably horrendous and unjustifiable evil.

They ignore the fact that the United States government fought one of the bloodiest wars in history to end slavery. They say the Civil War was fought for economic reasons with the aim of establishing the supremacy of the industrial North over the agricultural South. There is some truth to this. It is not, however, the whole truth. The antislavery movement was a major factor in bringing about the war, and many northerners gave their lives to end what they considered a reprehensible practice.

As bad as slavery was, there was no wholesale genocide of black people. They were enslaved and exploited, but they were not starved and killed in large numbers. Southern plantations required workers, not victims. Without excusing the excesses—the splitting up of families, the forced labor, the whippings—it should be understood that slaves were regarded as valuable property whose work output was more important to their owners than lashing or beating them.

Blacks and Jews Together

Holocaust revisionists also equate post-emancipation discrimination against blacks with anti-Semitic measures in Hitler's Germany. They point out that before the civil-rights era of the late 1950s and 1960s, there were many laws in the United States that stamped black Americans as second-class citizens. This cannot be denied. They were not allowed to serve alongside whites in the armed services; they were assigned to segregated units; in the navy they were assigned to lowly tasks such as kitchen duties. Many southern states had poll-tax laws designed to prevent blacks from voting. Other state and local laws kept blacks from swimming in public pools with whites, relegated them to the balconies of movie theaters and the rear areas of buses, segregated them so that they were barred from white-only public facilities and forced to use inferior rest rooms and drinking fountains, and in general dictated their rights and behavior in terms designed to define and maintain their inferiority.

The deniers insist that Hitler was right when he repeatedly boasted that he "treated Jews in Germany better than Negroes were treated in the United States." They point to a 1936 speech by Congressman Hamilton Fish in which he reported that "five thousand [African] Americans have been lynched in the last 50 years in this great free country of ours, that is supposed to be the most civilized in the world." They remind us that before the end of World War II anti-lynching legislation had repeatedly been voted down in the United States Congress.[10]

How was this any different from Germany's attitude toward Jews? ask the Holocaust revisionists. Is it not true, they add, that blacks are still discriminated against in many ways in the United States today? How dare we, they wonder, adopt a holier-than-thou attitude?

Some black people echo this point of view. Understandably bitter, they wonder how the sins of slavery and the persecution of black Americans can be disregarded while the genocide of the Jews results in public sympathy and Holocaust museums. Their bitterness provides fertile ground for Holocaust denial, and in some cases for outright anti-Semitism.

Nevertheless, it is doubtful that the majority of black people fall into this trap. They recognize that Jews also have been persecuted in the United States over the years. They know that Jews were the first whites to join in the struggle for civil rights. They have not forgotten Jews like Michael Schwerner and Andrew Goodman who—together with African American James E. Chaney—lost their lives in that struggle in 1964.

Most black leaders recognize that Hitler lied when he talked about how well he treated the Jews compared to the mistreatment of blacks in the United States. They know that the ill treatment of black Americans cannot excuse the Nazis' murder of six million Jews. They know that today's Holocaust deniers and white supremacists are cut from the same cloth. They know that the civil-rights battles still to be won for black people in the United States will not be won by Holocaust deniers, but rather by blacks and whites, including Jews, standing together in the struggle for equality for all.

Hiroshima, Nagasaki, and the Holocaust

From comparing the persecution of black Americans to the fate of Jews in Europe, the Holocaust deniers move on to excuse the latter by claiming that both sides were guilty of mass killings during World War II. Both sides dropped bombs, they remind us. Both sides killed civilians, including children. What morality, they ask, was there in the British carpet bombings of nonmilitary targets like Cologne, where 2,000 tons of bombs were dropped, and Dresden, in which 130,000 German civilians were killed? The 1942 bombing of Tokyo by U. S. planes is also pointed out as an example of dropping bombs on civilians to shake their morale, rather than targeting Japanese munitions plants and military targets.

Unnecessary as such bombings may have been, however, they cannot compare with the state-authorized murder of six million Jewish men, women, and children. More troubling are the questions the deniers raise about the dropping of atomic bombs on the Japanese cities of Hiroshima and Nagasaki. The first such bomb was dropped by a U. S. aircraft on Hiroshima on August 6, 1945. More than 100,000 people were immediately killed. Within five years the death toll from the radiation released by the bomb reached 200,000.

Three days later, while the Japanese government was considering the terms of surrender, a second atomic bomb was dropped on Nagasaki. The initial death toll was 70,000. Within five years it had grown to 140,000.

It was necessary to drop these deadly missiles according to those who ordered the bombings. It was either that or fight a series of island-by-island battles in the Pacific, which, it was estimated, would have cost one million American lives. Supreme Commander of Allied Forces in the Pacific General

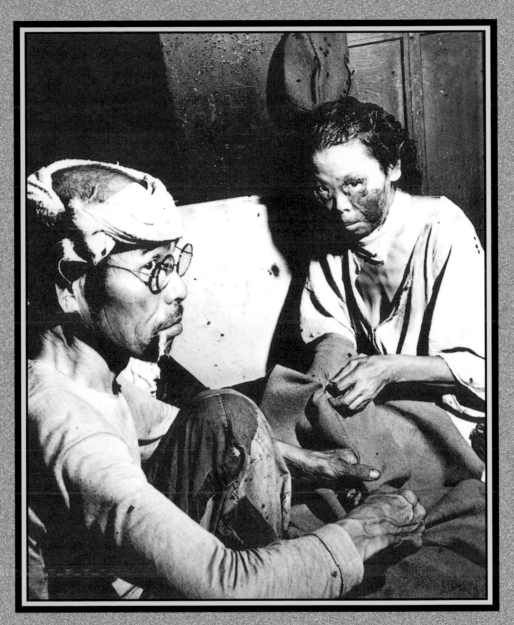

Two months after the destruction of Hiroshima by an atomic bomb, survivors sit in a damaged bank building converted into a makeshift hospital.

Douglas MacArthur disagreed. He did not think the bomb had been "of any military use against Japan." General (later president) Dwight Eisenhower thought "the Japanese were ready to surrender and it wasn't necessary to hit them with that awful thing."[11]

Holocaust deniers—and others not associated with them—particularly question the dropping of the second bomb on Nagasaki. After Hiroshima, the Japanese were ready to surrender. If there really was a genocide of Jews in Europe, deniers ask, was Nagasaki not also a racially motivated genocide?

There may be some truth to this, but—again—it does not justify the methodical slaughter of the Holocaust. The atomic bombings were acts of war. The Holocaust was a deliberate and ongoing extermination of innocents. Americans do not deny dropping the atomic bombs. They immediately took responsibility for helping the survivors. The Holocaust revisionists, however, do deny the deeds of the Nazis. They continue pursuing an anti-Semitic agenda with the aim of reviving Nazism and creating a *Judenrein* world.

Every country has shameful chapters in its history. Hiroshima and Nagasaki may well be a blot on the history of the United States. The shame of nations is not reserved for Germany alone. Redemption, however, can only come from facing the past, not from denying it.

The second business deal . . . concerned the delivery of articles of value of dead Jews to the Reichsbank [Nazi Germany's national bank]. . . . the objects to be delivered were the jewelry and valuables of concentration camp inmates, especially of Jews, who had been killed in extermination camps. The objects in question were rings, watches, eyeglasses, ingots of gold, wedding rings, brooches, pins, frames of glasses, foreign currency and other valuables. . . . It was an enormous quantity of valuables, since there was a steady flow of deliveries for months and years.[1]

—SS *Obergruppenführer* Oswald Pohl,
testifying at the 1946 Nuremberg war crimes trials,
where he was subsequently sentenced to death

he Nazis were not only slaughterers. They were also colossal thieves. This thievery was supervised by Reichmarschall Hermann Göring, second in command to Adolf Hitler. On September 17, 1940, Göring had ordered the seizure of "movable and immovable property, stores and intangible interests of Jews. . . ."[2] Nobody knows how many millions—perhaps billions—of dollars worth of property was stolen by the Nazis.

The Nazi Art Collector

Göring did not steal only for the Nazis; he stole for himself. He boasted of being an art collector. When the German army occupied Paris in 1940, Göring ordered that the "Jewish art property" seized by the invaders should either be reserved for Hitler at his command, or reserved for "the completion of the Reich Marshal's [Göring's] collection." He arranged for those "confiscated Jewish art treasures," which he had selected for himself and Hitler to be "loaded on two railroad cars which will be attached to the Reich Marshal's special train" bound for Berlin.[3]

Nazi records show that "from March, 1941, to July, 1944, 29 large shipments of pictorial art [mostly paintings] were brought into the Reich [Germany] comprising 137 freight cars containing 4,174 cases of art works. . . . By July, 1944, a total of 21,903 art objects of all types . . . had been counted and inventoried."[4] The total value of these works of art is impossible to estimate.

Some of this art was sold, some was traded, and some was auctioned off. Göring was involved in many transactions in which ten or eleven works by minor artists were traded to art dealers for a major work by Titian or Rembrandt. In France much modern art, viewed as "degenerate" by the Nazis, was "taken from five Jewish families who were prominent art dealers." Because they were regarded as depraved and not worth holding onto, many works by modern artists such as Degas, Monet, Renoir, Gauguin, van Gogh, and Picasso were sold "on the international art market—some leaving Europe via neutral Switzerland."[5]

Fifty years later, sales and trades such as these created a nightmare for the art world as original owners, or their heirs, began to discover their property in shops, galleries, and even museums. A Manhattan court impounded two paintings by Austrian expressionist Egon Schiele, which had been on display at the world-renowned Museum of Modern Art, when relatives of Holocaust survivors—the original owners—claimed the paintings. Prominent art houses like Sotheby's and Christie's have been accused of not checking the legitimacy of Nazi-stolen, Jewish-owned paintings they have put up for auction.

According to the Holocaust deniers, the Nazis didn't steal the works of art in question, they bought them. They argue that "the German government had a keen interest in bringing as much Germanic art as possible back under German protection." They add that "the Germans often had agreements with Jewish art dealers, swapping the modern paintings they weren't interested in for the Germanic paintings they were interested in." They accuse the Jews of engaging "in a huge treasure hunt for those paintings now in Gentile [non-Jewish] hands which formerly belonged to Jews." The deniers insist that "there are statutes of limitations for such claims."[6] What they are saying is that after a certain period of time crimes such as art thefts cannot legally be prosecuted. But

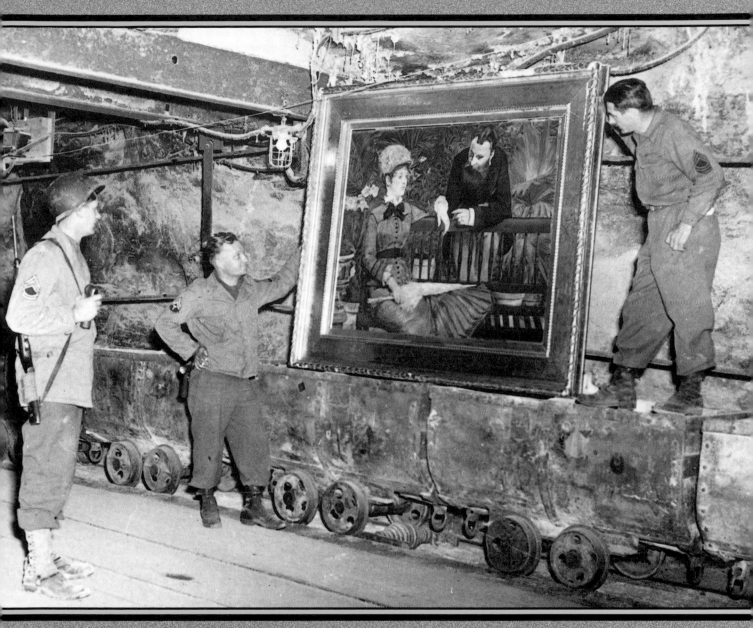

Discovered in a German salt mine by U.S. soldiers, this painting by Édouard Manet was only one of the countless treasures stolen by the Nazis from their wealthier victims.

this isn't true. Under international law, there is no statute of limitations for the crimes committed by the Nazis.

Deniers Reject Atonement

Even if there was a statute of limitations for Holocaust crimes, it would not have been in effect on September 27, 1951—six years after the end of World War II— when the West German parliament unanimously voted to make reparations to the Jewish people. Konrad Adenauer, then the chancellor, said that the people of Germany "had the obligation to make moral and material amends . . . for the unspeakable crimes committed in the name of the German people."[7] Payments, the parliament had decided, would be made to both individual Jewish survivors and to the Jewish nation of Israel.

Holocaust deniers were outraged back then—as they are now—at the idea that Germany should pay any money to Jews. Their claim is that the Holocaust was invented by Jews "to blackmail West Germany into 'atoning' with the twenty billion dollars of indemnities [payments] to Israel."[8] Actually, the agreement was for $822 million, not $20 billion. According to the *Encyclopedia of the Holocaust,* only $110 million went to Israel directly. The rest was parceled out to satisfy individual claims by survivors and by the families of those who were killed.

Because it doesn't fit in with their propaganda of a Holocaust invented for profit by money-hungry Jews, the deniers persist in misstating the basis for the payments. They insist that "the size of the German reparations to Israel has been based on the theory that vast numbers of Jews were exterminated . . . some six million being the most usually accepted number."[9] In fact, the government of Israel based its 1951 claim "on the basis of total expenditures already made and the expenditure still needed for the integration of Jewish immigrants from Nazi-dominated countries"—not on the basis of the six million murdered in the Holocaust.[10]

The "Max Heliger" Account

Gold—because it retains its value in a way that paper currency may not—was particularly lusted after by the Nazis. In the death camps, gold fillings were pulled from the teeth of murdered Jews. German firms like "I. G. Farben, the Krupp Werke and Siemens-Schuckert Werke had established plants in Auschwitz as well as near the Lublin death camps."[11] The gold was melted down in their facilities and shipped to a bank where it was deposited to a secret account under the name "Max Heliger."

Most of the Jews who were herded into ghettoes before being shipped to death camps had believed that they were going to be resettled in some better place when they were moved the second time. They had been urged to bring whatever jewelry they owned with them. They also brought whatever money they had. After their deaths, the money and the valuables were also deposited in the Max Heliger account.

Eventually assets from the Max Heliger account, as well as other holdings seized from the Jews by the Nazis, were transferred to special Swiss bank accounts. During World War II, Switzerland was a neutral country, and Swiss bank accounts have traditionally been shielded by law from investigation. Although the Nazis kept records of their holdings in Swiss banks, some lawsuits by Jews to reclaim this money have dragged on for years. The claimants have had to follow an involved paper trail, which Holocaust deniers claim is made up of forgeries.

Swiss Bank Accounts

The paper trail leading to Swiss banks also involves Jews who claim accounts opened by themselves, or members of their families, in order to keep their funds and valuables out of the hands of the Nazis. In the 1930s, before World War II, Jews who tried to leave Germany, including the few who succeeded, were forbidden to take their money with them. Many, often with the help of non-Jewish friends, managed to smuggle money out of the country and deposit it in Swiss banks under false names. Following the same procedure, valuables were placed for safekeeping in safety deposit boxes in Swiss banks. In the confusion of the war, many of the records of such accounts were lost, stolen, or destroyed.

Jewish groups claimed that as much as $7 billion of Jewish assets, including money and gold deposited by the Nazis, was still held by Swiss banks. The Swiss Bankers Association (SBA) initially insisted it had located only $32 million in unclaimed accounts. In 1996, Jean-Pascal Delamuraz, then the president of Switzerland, said that the survivors' demands were "nothing less than extortion and blackmail."[12]

Since then, Holocaust deniers have quoted this statement over and over again to show that a legitimate head of state has embraced their view. They do not mention that a short time later, in January 1997, former president Delamuraz took back the statement and issued an apology. Instead they insist that the Swiss "are dealing with Ghetto-gangster elements in pin-striped suits who carry calculators in their violin cases, rather than Thompson machine guns," adding that "the take of their terrorism is far more lucrative than if they had used guns."

In the end, a settlement was reached by which the Swiss banks paid back $1.25 billion to satisfy legitimate Jewish claims. Sadly, in October 1999, "for the first time in history Switzerland's rightwing conservative People's Party (SVP) . . . . won more votes than any other party."[13] The party is backed by billionaire Christoph Blocher, who has praised the work of Jurgen Graf, a Swiss revisionist who repeatedly denies that the Holocaust took place.

Payment for Slave Labor

An issue even thornier than Swiss bank accounts is the use by Nazi Germany's major manufacturing companies of slave laborers—mostly Jews. These former slave laborers—or their heirs—are now asking payment for the work that was done. As Nazi documents bear out, it was done under horrendous conditions. Prisoners were beaten and starved and received no medical treatment. They were literally worked to death. Now reparations have been sought for their suffering` and their labor.

The basis of these suits is the relationship between the companies, the Nazi government, and the concentration camps, which supplied the slave laborers. It is established by industry documents and Nazi records. As with other such documentation, the Holocaust deniers claim these are forgeries. As usual, they claim that war crimes trial testimony by the Nazis involved was elicited by torture, and that survivor testimony is dictated by what they call the Zionist conspiracy.

On July 7, 2000, the German government and the companies involved reached an agreement with United States negotiators to pay $5 billion into a fund for former Jewish slave laborers or their heirs. The Holocaust deniers claim that both governments continue to be manipulated by Zionist infiltrators. In their view, Jews exercise vast control over most of the non-Arab governments of the world. This is an echo of the world conspiracy theory of the discredited hundred-year-old *Protocols of the Learned Elders of Zion.*

The Legality of War Crimes Trials

Many of the reparations claims are based on evidence and testimony presented at the war crimes trials held in Nuremberg and elsewhere following World War II. Over and over again—relying on Hitler's stated belief that repetition of the big lie will eventually persuade people—the Holocaust deniers insist that the documents put in evidence at the trials were forgeries and that the incriminating testimony was obtained by torture. They repeat and repeat that the trials were a Jewish-engineered conspiracy.

Then they go beyond that in a campaign to prove that the war crimes trials were illegal. The deniers say they were "based upon a complete disregard of sound legal precedents, principles and procedures. The court had no real jurisdiction over the accused or their offenses . . . it permitted the accusers to act as prosecutors, judges, jury and executioners; and it admitted to the group of prosecutors those who had been guilty of crimes as numerous and atrocious as those with which the accused were charged." They offer no proof of this, nor of their conclusion that "these trials degraded international jurisprudence as never before in human experience."[14]

If their argument was to be accepted, trials for modern-day atrocities committed in Bosnia, Rwanda, Cambodia, and other places would have no validity. They could not be held. There would be no way that society could impose the rule of law on crimes against humanity. This would be the ultimate victory of the Holocaust deniers, and the ultimate defeat of civilization.

THE ROLE OF THE INTERNET

7

Congress shall make no law respecting an establishment of religion, or prohibiting the free exercise thereof; or abridging the freedom of speech, or of the press, or the right of the people peaceably to assemble, and to petition the Government for a redress of grievances.[1]

—Article I of the Bill of Rights of the U.S. Constitution

Under Article I of the Bill of Rights (usually referred to as the First Amendment), a series of Supreme Court decisions has affirmed that "hate speech . . . is permitted as long as the speech does not constitute 'fighting words.'" These are words which "inflict injury or tend to incite an immediate breach of peace." Some people argue that hate speech fits the definition of fighting words. Others point out that a person sitting at a computer isn't likely to be provoked into immediate violence by reading a hate message. Either way, however, the message is offensive and psychologically harmful.[2]

Hundreds of Internet Hate Sites

The First Amendment does not protect speech that foments violence against Jews or blacks or other ethnic minorities. However, it does insist that the threat be direct and imminent. Justice Oliver Wendell Holmes Jr. believed that "freedom for the thought that we hate" was the most important principle in the Constitution.[3]

Distributing information that may be untrue such as Holocaust denial is not forbidden by the First Amendment. Those alarmed by the viciousness of hate speech on the Internet argue that "the rights of victims of hate speech have been subordinated to rights of freedom of speech."[4] This is confirmed, they say, by the growing number of hate sites.

At present, according to Anti-Defamation League (ADL) testimony before the United States Senate Committee on the Judiciary, "hundreds of bigotry-laden sites [are] on the Web." They "target the young [and are] aimed at influencing both attitudes and behavior." Some organizations, "such as the World Church of the Creator, have posted Web sites filled with simple propaganda devoted specifically to wooing children."[5]

A Two-Way Street

Holocaust denial is not always the main point of hate sites on the Internet. They embrace a variety of bigoted and paranoid views. These run the gamut from anti-immigrant, antigay, anti-Semitic, and white supremacist positions to antigovernment propaganda for armed militias.

These groups, however, have noted the success of the Holocaust deniers in attracting followers. Hate mongers embrace Holocaust denial as a tool to attract more people—particularly young people—to their own Internet sites. They have learned that it is a series of very short steps from Holocaust denial to anti-Semitism to white supremacy to hating a government that grants equality to nonwhites and non-Christians, to other fanatic programs, many of which lead to violence.

It's a two-way street. Members of these groups are also converted to Holocaust denial. That is one reason the number of sites specifically devoted to Holocaust denial grew from three in 1996 to more than a dozen in 1999. They generate "thousands of pages of propaganda on the Web."[6] Hitler's theory that "the great masses of the people . . . will more easily fall victims to a big lie," if it is repeated often enough, gains new momentum through the Internet where the lie denying the Holocaust can now reach a potentially worldwide audience.[7]

A Historical Truth

The targeting of children and young adults is no accident. The Holocaust occurred more than half a century ago. Not only children and adolescents, but also most of their parents have no memory of it. The reality and the horror have faded away. It is all too easy with the passage of time to view the Holocaust through the mists of history and wonder if it really happened. What is wrong, ask the deniers, with questioning that? Isn't there room for reasonable people to discuss whether the Holocaust was real, or invented by the Jews for sympathy or profit?

No, there isn't. While there may be room for raising questions in history, certain events are so momentous, and so supported by the evidence, that to challenge them is to raise the question of the challenger's motives. World War II happened. The Civil War happened. Slavery existed in the United States. Atomic bombs were dropped on Hiroshima and Nagasaki. And six million European Jews died in the Holocaust.

The real purpose of denying the Holocaust was frankly admitted by Harold Covington of the National Socialist White People's Party in an E-mail message he sent out to the party's mailing list. "Take away the Holocaust," he enthused, and people would be "stunned with admiration for the brilliance of Adolf Hitler." The purpose of Holocaust denial, Covington added, is "to make National Socialism an acceptable political alternative again."[8]

The Ku Klux Klan Web site run by racist skinhead Reuben Longdon denies the Holocaust in order to attract people to their antiblack cause. The Klan has traditionally taken every opportunity to connect hatred of blacks with persecution of Jews, Catholics, and others. Indeed, Longdon has publicly admitted that he does not himself doubt that the Holocaust took place, but only posts Holocaust-denial material in order to attract those who swallow it to his cause. Such messages, targeting young people, open the door to another Holocaust—

A civil-rights lawyer for the Anti-Defamation League examines a white supremacist Web site.

one aimed not only at Jews, but at all non-Christians, blacks, Latinos, all non-white immigrants, gays and lesbians, and anybody else who opposes those who promote such views.

Hate Filters: Pro and Con

Should this bigotry targeting young people be permitted to be spread over the Internet? California Senator Dianne Feinstein doesn't think so. "This is not part of their First Amendment rights, this is the difference between free speech and teaching someone how to kill," she says.[9] Mary Ellen Gale of Whittier College School of Law agrees. She doesn't accept "the same set of platitudes that we have heard for so many years about the First Amendment trumping all other rights in the Constitution. We have a Fourteenth Amendment (which provides people equal protection under the law). We have a commitment to equality. It is time we made that commitment real."[10]

Such positions support installing so-called hate filters on the Internet. The Anti-Defamation League, using technology developed by Cyber Patrol, a division of the Learning Company in Cambridge, Massachusetts, has approved such a filter. When it is installed, a user who attempts to access a site that promotes bigotry will see a warning on the screen that says: "Hate Zone. Access Restricted." The user will also be directed to an ADL "Stop Hate" Internet site providing material about various kinds of bigotry.[11] An ADL spokesperson says the filter is intended to block out sites that advocate "hatred, bigotry or even violence toward Jews or other groups on the basis of their religion, race, ethnicity, [or] sexual orientation."[12] The definition includes Holocaust denial.

Not everybody believes that hate filters are a good idea. The American Civil Liberties Union (ACLU) insists that "to justify suppression of speech, the speech must be intended to produce imminent lawless action and must be likely to produce such action."[13] In other words, hate speech is only illegal if it directly provokes violence. It's very hard to prove that most Internet hate sites—and specifically Holocaust denial sites—fit that definition. The connection between logging onto a hate site and committing a hostile action is often too flimsy to pin down.

Mark Potok, editor of the Southern Poverty Law Center's Intelligence Project, expressed doubts that censorship filters could be both fair and effective. He feels that bigoted sites are a small percentage of total Internet sites "and it would be unfair to limit the freedom of so many because of so few."[14] There is also the problem of hate message sites closing down before they can be answered, and then reopening under a new Web site name.

Although the American Library Association opposes the use of hate filters, in practice their use is left up to individual library systems. Nevertheless, Karen G. Schneider, a librarian who has written a book about filters, says that she finds it "disturbing that the anti-Defamation League thinks that the way to prevent anti-Semitism is to hide it from the people who care about anti-Semitism." She believes that "there's nothing to make a bad idea look silly like putting it out in the cold, hard light of day."[15]

An International Problem

Those who advocate filters believe that Ms. Schneider has missed the gut-level emotional appeal of Holocaust denial sites and other hate sites to some young people and others who are not well-informed. Many of them are drawn to anti-establishment material because of their own inner needs or failings. The sites provide stirring martial music. They weave totally false, but thrilling, often violent, them-and-us tales in which good guys are being bullied by bad guys—rich, Communist Jews; violent, oversexed blacks; takeover-immigrant Latinos; papist Catholics; Wall Street brokers; and oppressive big government. The sites build a fellowship of those who think of themselves as underdogs oppressed by non-whites, non-Christians, and non-heterosexuals. They offer violent video games in which the opponent is a Jew, a gay, or a black, and the goal is to wipe out the enemy. Some even offer advice on obtaining weapons or building bombs.

It is an international problem. The Web site of the Charlemagne Hammerskins, a French group, displayed a man with a gun wearing a ski mask and standing alongside a swastika. A mouse click on "Access for sub-humans" revealed a concentration camp and the words, "We still have many one-way tickets for Auschwitz."[16] Another site, based in Sweden, questions the reality of the Holocaust and portrays caricatures of evil-looking Jews with long noses and scraggly black beards wearing Stars of David (Jewish religious symbols). By present estimates, there are more than eight hundred anti-Semitic and racist sites on the World Wide Web.

Concern over such Internet sites was so great that in November 1997 a United Nations Internet Hate Speech Conference was convened in Geneva, Switzerland. The conference chairperson, Agha Shahi of Pakistan, reminded those attending that 148 countries had signed a global treaty against racial discrimination. He said that hate sites were violating that treaty, and that the countries who signed it had an obligation to enact measures to eliminate hate sites.

Some countries already had such laws on the books. Earlier in 1997, Germany had brought charges against the Internet service provider Compuserve for making accessible computer games "that glorify violence and contain Nazi symbols."[17] As a result, Compuserve shut down such sites. However, closing down the sites isn't always effective. A French Holocaust revisionist site that was shut down in France opened under a different name in Sweden with a more inflammatory message than ever. In Europe, border jumping by hate groups is common. Even so, most of the hate pages are based on Internet service providers located in the United States.

What Are Rights? What Is Right?

There is protection for the hate sites in the United States. Legally, the First Amendment to the Constitution shields them. In 1996 the Senate passed the Communications Decency Act to protect children from unsavory material on the Internet. Its main purpose was to guard against pornographic sites, but a vaguely worded provision was aimed at hate sites as well. However, on June 26, 1997, the Supreme Court struck down the act, saying that it violated the First Amendment's guarantee of freedom of speech.

It follows that while the United States signed the UN document prohibiting discrimination, the government's position is that it will not pass laws infringing on free speech. Despite this, a new bill pending in the Senate would require Internet service providers with more than 50,000 subscribers to provide them with filtering software free, or at cost, within three years. The bill is cosponsored by Republican Senator Orrin Hatch of Utah and Democratic Senator Patrick Leahy of Vermont, two of the Senate's most powerful leaders.

Opposition is already building to the new bill. Both the ACLU and People for the American Way have posted messages opposing it on their Web sites. The organization for Morality in Media has also come out against it. The nonlegal argument of those who oppose the bill is that the Holocaust deniers and other hate mongers "need attention, ignore them and they slither back under their rock." To which a Holocaust survivor might reply, "I've heard this talk before. But it wasn't here in America, it was back in Germany in the late '20s."[18] The implication is that it can happen again, and it can happen here in the United States.

The questions regarding Holocaust denial on the Internet remain unanswered. Should a limit defined by ethics and truth be imposed on the First Amendment right of free speech? Or would that limit be the first step toward giving up our constitutional rights as Americans?

DENIERS, HATERS & KILLERS

8

False words are not only evil in themselves, but they infect the soul with evil.[1]

—Plato, philosopher of ancient Greece

he violence of hatred is a chain made up of many links. Some Holocaust deniers cloak themselves in academic respectability. Some are openly anti-Semitic, but claim to deplore violence. Some disguise their anti-Semitism as religious principle. Some embrace theories of racial purity and extend their anti-Semitism to persecute African Americans, Asian Americans, and Latinos. Some proudly proclaim themselves neo-Nazis and embrace Hitler's theories of race purity and Aryan superiority. Some follow the road from Holocaust denial to justifying violence. Some commit violence. Some kill.

A Wake-up Call

One confessed killer is thirty-seven-year-old hate group member Buford O'Neal Furrow, who walked into a Los Angeles Jewish community center in August 1999 and fired seventy bullets from a semiautomatic weapon. He wounded five people—three young boys, a sixty-eight-year-old receptionist, and a teenage camp counselor. One of the victims, a five-year-old, was seriously wounded. None of the victims died, but Furrow didn't know that when he subsequently walked into a Las Vegas office of the FBI and told them, "You're looking for me—I killed the kids in Los Angeles." He said he did it as "a wake-up call to America to kill Jews."[2]

The way authorities piece together the story, an hour after leaving the community center, Furrow shot and killed thirty-nine-year-old Joseph Ileto, a Filipino-American mailman who was just starting to walk his route in the Los Angeles suburb of Chatsworth. Furrow allegedly fired several bullets into Ileto's body. Furrow told the FBI that he had killed Ileto because of his race.

Furrow embraced the doctrine of the Christian Identity movement, which rates "No. 1 on the FBI's list of most dangerous hate groups."[3] According to their teachings, Jews are "children of Satan,"[4] and nonwhites are "'mudpeople' who must be exterminated."[5] Christian Identity is a sort of umbrella organization providing a bigoted philosophy and a call to action for groups such as the Ku Klux Klan, the Aryan Nation, The Order, and others. It provides followers with assurances that they are acting "under the authority of 'God's Law.'"[6] One of their activities is spreading the lies of Holocaust deniers.

The Order

Furrow had a history of anti-Semitism with different hate groups. At the beginning of the 1990s he belonged to The Order and had a relationship with Debbie Matthews, widow of The Order founder, Robert J. Matthews. Matthews had been killed in a shootout with federal agents following an armored truck holdup in California in 1984. That same year members of The Order had been involved in the killing of Jewish radio talk-show host Alan Berg in Denver.

Berg's murder had been a "carefully planned paramilitary operation funded with bank robbery proceeds." The Order had compiled a "hate list" of those they considered "threatening [to] the existence of the white race."[7] On the list were Henry Kissinger, David Rockefeller, Fred Silverman, and Alan Berg. The only one on the list who was actually targeted and killed was Berg. He had been an outspoken opponent of anti-Semitic and racist groups.

Throughout the 1980s, The Order was the most violent of the hate groups. Indeed, it went so far as to lay plans for the overthrow of the United States government. By the 1990s, however, it had become somewhat inactive, and many of its members had left it for the Aryan Nation—an Idaho-based paramilitary neo-Nazi organization. A giant swastika is painted on the corrugated roof of one of the buildings of its barbed-wire-enclosed compound in Hayden Lake, Idaho. A "Whites only" sign is nailed to a tree near the gate.[8]

Buford Furrow was a security guard there. Mark Potok of the Southern Poverty Law Center has a photo of Furrow in a Nazi uniform that was taken at the compound in 1995. There is evidence, however, that the Aryan Nations weren't quite militant enough for Furrow, and that it was his ambition to join a more violent top-secret hate group that pushed him into shooting the children at the community center. The name of this group is Phineas Priests.

Phineas Priests

Phineas Priests are right-wing white supremacists and anti-Semites. Most of them believe in Christian Identity teaching, including Holocaust denial. What mainly separates Phineas Priests from other hate groups is the frequency with which they engage in violent action. Indeed, it is the commission of an act of violence that defines one as a Phineas Priest.

Some of these acts—like Furrow's—are done by individuals acting on their own to promote the organization's beliefs and so prove their worthiness to become a Phineas Priest. Others are done by small cells—no more than six-man teams. (Women are excluded from joining the Phineas Priesthood.) These teams are part of "a tactic promoted by white supremacists and militia organizers called 'leaderless resistance.'"[9]

Bank robber Walter Eliyah Thody, whose gangly frame and scraggly beard give him the look of a zealous prophet from biblical times, is a Phineas Priest who sees himself as a soldier of God. "Killing is normally murder," he admits. "Theft is theft. But if you're in warfare, then those same acts are acts of war. I'm at warfare against the enemies of my country."[10]

Violence as a Recruiting Tool

The soldiers in the war being waged by Phineas Priests have a symbol, usually worn as a belt buckle, in which a cross is rounded at the top to form the letter p above a number symbol [#] and the numeral 25. The symbol refers to Chapter 25, the Book of Numbers in the Old Testament of the Bible. The biblical story found there tells of how a man "enters into an unlawful union with a woman from another tribe" and brings down God's wrath upon his people for doing so. "Phineas kills the race-mixing couple and thus appeases God."[11] It is this act, which today we might call terrorist, that the Phineas Priest is called upon to emulate.

One of the first, and possibly the most famous to do so was Byron de la Beckwith, who murdered civil-rights activist Medgar Evers in 1963. More recently, another was Paul Hill, who in 1993 wrote an essay advocating "Phineas actions" and the following year went out and killed a doctor and his security escort at an abortion clinic in Pensacola, Florida. Calling themselves the Aryan Republican Army (ARA), self-styled Phineas terrorists Peter Kevin Langan and Richard Lee Gutherie were charged in Ohio with committing twenty-two bank robberies between January 1994 and January 1996. (Gutherie hanged himself in his jail cell.) An office of the newspaper *Spokesman Review* was firebombed in Spokane, Washington, and littered with Phineas literature. In 1996 notes referring to the Phineas Priesthood were left at the scenes of two bank robberies and three firebombings in Spokane. In Idaho Falls, Idaho, threatening flyers of the Phineas Priesthood were left on the cars of churchgoing Unitarians while they were attending Sunday services. The flyers warned that "names and addresses of law violators are being compiled. . . . Soon the fog that comes from Heaven will be accompanied by the destroying wind of a righteous God."[12]

Violence and threats of violence by Phineas Priests are viewed by hate groups as a magnet to attract new members. Matthew Hale, founder of the World Church of the Creator, sees violence as a recruiting tool. Murder and other acts of violence, in his view, "increase the notoriety of the church, and in a sense, no publicity is bad publicity." The insidious message of hate groups masquerading under the cloak of religion promises new recruits "membership in an elite army for God."[13]

California's Nazi Lowriders

A different sort of message is being offered by the Nazi Lowriders gang, described in an Anti-Defamation League report based on state and federal crime data as "the fastest-growing white supremacist gang in California and a major player in the methamphetamine drug trade."[14] The Nazi Lowriders embrace the whole gamut of anti-Semitic propaganda from Holocaust denial to theories of Jewish world domination. The biggest threat they pose, however, is their campaign to unite other white supremacist groups under their banner. Their efforts at recruitment are one of the reasons they have been segregated from other prisoners in the jails of Los Angeles County and Orange County.

These recruitment efforts evidently work. It attracted skinheads—right-wing rebels who reject society, shave their heads, and characteristically embrace random violence as a way of life. Nazi Lowriders membership grew from 28 in 1996 to approximately 1,300 in 1998. "They are not typical of skinhead organizations and not well defined like the Ku Klux Klan or Aryan Nations," according to the Center for Democratic Renewal (CDR), which monitors hate groups. "They are roving gangs," known as "'street soldiers.' They hit and they leave and they are hard to track and pin down."[15]

Nazi Lowriders used a metal pipe to beat up a twelve-year-old Latino boy at a video arcade, according to police. In another incident, they beat an African-American teenager with a baseball bat. They also repeatedly stabbed a black man in the back. Although "they express hatred for Jews, Asians and other minorities," their violence is focused mainly on blacks.[16] Ganging up on blacks is another reason they have been segregated in prison.

Like other hate group propaganda, the Nazi Lowriders message primarily attracts males in their late teens or early twenties. A sort of clubhouse mentality involving hand signals, secret language, and dress codes prevails. "Members' bodies," according to the CDR, "are often tattooed with swastikas, pictures of Adolf Hitler and other Nazi imagery."[17] But they are neo-Nazis with a difference. Their drug-selling expertise has made them a force to be reckoned with in Southern California narcotics trafficking.

Consider Austria

Nazi Lowriders and other hate groups are still on the fringes in the United States. They are not part of mainstream American life. In Europe that is not always the case. In many European countries Holocaust denial and its anti-Semitic message are spreading. Nowhere has this been demonstrated so clearly as in Austria.

It may be relevant that before and during World War II, Austria was a willing partner of the Nazis. In a vote held on April 10, 1938, 99 percent of the voters in Austria and Germany approved the union of the two countries. According to "reliable estimates" cited by *Commentary* magazine: "Austrians composed as much as 40 percent of those most intensively involved in the Nazi genocide."[18] In other words, the Holocaust was the work of Austrians as well as Germans.

But that was in the past. It makes no more sense to blame today's Austrians for the Holocaust than it makes to blame today's Germans. It was another generation, another world, and the hatred generated by the deeds of the Nazis can only generate more hatred and more violence if it is embraced today. It is not Austria's Nazi past, but Austria's more recent present which is of concern.

Waldheim and Haider

Between 1972 and 1981, the secretary-general of the United Nations was Austria's representative, Kurt Waldheim. In March 1986 it was revealed that

Waldheim had participated during World War II "in the torture of Yugoslavian Jews and the deportation of thousands of Greek Jews" to concentration camps.[19] Two months later he was elected president of Austria by a large margin of votes. His opponent, Dr. Kurt Steyer, said that "anti-Semitic sentiment" among Austrians was decisive in the election.[20] When, in 1987, the Justice Department cited Waldheim's Nazi past as reason to bar him from entering the United States, Waldheim blamed American Jews for his exclusion.

In the same year that Waldheim was elected president of Austria, 1986, Jorg Haider became the leader of Austria's Freedom Party. The Freedom Party had been established in 1956, and from the first it catered to the interests of former Austrian Nazis. Haider has carried on the party's program of Holocaust denial. He and the party have often "questioned, trivialized, or whitewashed" the Nazi genocide of the Jews. Haider has called the SS, who carried out much of the Holocaust, "decent fellows." He refers to extermination camps as "punishment camps," and praises many of the policies of Hitler's Third Reich.[21]

Haider is the owner of a 38,000-acre estate, which Nazis forced a Jewish widow to sell to his family for a fraction of its value in 1940. In 1979 he was first elected to the Austrian parliament as a Freedom Party representative. Subsequently he was elected governor of the Austrian province of Carinthia. Throughout his career he has championed the anti-immigrant cause of "Austria for the Austrians." He has spoken of Austria's need to preserve its *Lebensraum* (living space). His choice of words often resembles the language used in the Nazi party propaganda of the 1930s.

Coalition and Sanctions

In October 1999 the Freedom Party came in second in Austria's national election, winning 27 percent of the vote. Since the first-place party had not won a majority, the Freedom Party was able to unite with the right-wing People's Party, which had finished third, to form a coalition to rule Austria. Although Haider himself did not take a position in the national government (he continued as governor of Carinthia), the Freedom Party took over half the seats in the cabinet, and the widespread perception was that Haider was running the country.

This led the fourteen member nations of the European Union to impose economic sanctions against Austria, to cut off diplomatic relations by boycotting Austrian ambassadors, and to scale back cultural exchanges. Following a mass demonstration against Freedom Party policies by 200,000 Viennese Austrians in February 2000, Haider resigned as head of the Freedom Party. However, the European Union members dismissed his resignation as a tactical maneuver and continued the sanctions against Austria.

Many Austrians regard the Freedom Party as thinly disguised neo-Nazis. Nevertheless, the party continues to enjoy sufficient support to stay in power. Most alarmingly, surveys taken in Germany show that 36 percent of the German people say they agree either "totally" or "in many respects" with Haider.

The Prize and the Message

A reflection of such German sentiment in the academic community was the June 2000 award of the Konrad Adenauer Prize for literature by the Deutschland Foundation to Ernst Nolte, a historian who justifies the Holocaust. In his acceptance speech, Nolte said that "Nazism was the 'strongest of all counter forces' to Bolshevism [Russian communism], a movement with wide Jewish support," adding that "Hitler may have had 'rational' reasons for attacking the Jews." Harvard historian Charles Maier charges that "the award of the prize to Nolte was a clear political statement intended to promote the view that there is no particular stigma to Nazism." According to *The New York Times*, Jorg Haider's rise in Austria has created fertile ground for his views in Germany where there is "anger, at what is seen as Germany's eternal victimization for the Holocaust."[22]

A few days after receiving the Adenauer Prize, Ernst Nolte addressed a conference in Paris. Here he again justified Hitler's anti-Semitic programs. His

Austrian Jorg Haider campaigning for the Freedom Party in September 1999

French audience applauded him enthusiastically. In France the National Front of Holocaust denier Jean-Marie Le Pen is growing. France also is the home of the late Robert Faurisson, one of the earliest Holocaust deniers whose theories are still widely quoted by other deniers. Faurisson was tried and convicted in a French court of "incitement to racial hatred and violence."[23]

France is neither alone in having laws against Holocaust denial nor in having hate groups which are anti-immigration, anti-people of color, and anti-Semitic. Not only Austria and Germany, but Switzerland, Denmark, Belgium, England, Australia, Canada, and many other industrialized countries have laws against Holocaust denial as well as groups of organized bigots. The United States has no such laws, but we do have hate groups.

Their numbers are small, but they are a threat. As we have seen, the hate mongers often try to rewrite Holocaust history with the aim of shaping future events. However, the future belongs to us. We must not let them take it away.

AFTERWORD

From *The Apocrypha*, sacred literature
of the ancient Alexandrian Jews

Although neither deniers nor revisionists raise legitimate questions about the Holocaust, there are nevertheless legitimate questions to be raised about Holocaust denial. Should freedom of speech include the freedom to tell lies? Who decides what is true and what is a lie? Should the young and impressionable be exposed to propaganda deliberately designed to make them hate others? If we deny the deniers the right to spread their venom, are we then putting our own right to free speech at risk? At which point does hate speech so directly provoke violence that it should be banned?

If young people are to learn, it has been said, then they must ask questions. Should this include questioning the established facts of history—both ancient and modern? Should it include questioning the reality of the Crusades, the Moorish conquests? European colonialism? American slavery? The bombing of Pearl Harbor? The Vietnam War? Genocide in Rwanda? Cambodia? Bosnia? The Holocaust?

What about the pain of those who survived the Holocaust? Of those who lost parents, brothers and sisters, husbands, wives, children, whole families? Should their pain be denied because reality is up for grabs?

Is it realistic to view Holocaust denial as the gateway to another Holocaust? Is the Holocaust a weapon to dump blame and guilt on the entire populations of nations? Must the post-Holocaust generation of Germans, Austrians, Poles,

Ukrainians, and others accept responsibility for atrocities that occurred long before they were born? Is this legitimate, or is it merely another version of group hatred?

These are difficult questions. Holocaust denial is not, however, a reasonable answer. Those who believe they must consider the claims of the deniers should do so. However, they must also consider the overwhelming evidence that the Holocaust really happened. The Jews and other victims didn't make it up. They were slaughtered because of unreasonable hatred. Looking into Holocaust denial must not excuse efforts to rekindle that hatred.

The quest for truth begins with doubt. But curiosity must not be satisfied with the venom of half-truths and lies. Facts are valid; distortions are not. All truth is precious, and the truth of the Holocaust is particularly so. It says that the six million Jews did not die in vain.

A German Poet's Truth

Ursula Duba was a Christian child growing up in Germany during the Nazi years of World War II. Today she is a poet. Holocaust denial is perhaps best answered in this poem by her:

> *the stain*
> *caused by*
> *the one and a half million Jewish children*
> *starved to death gassed*
> *or shot as target practice*
> *the four and a half million adult Jews*
> *the hundreds of thousands of Gypsies*
> *the Jehovah's Witnesses*
> *the mentally and physically disabled*
> *murdered*
> *cannot be expunged*[2]

SOURCE NOTES

Chapter One

1. Georges Braque, *Pensées sur l'Art,* in *Bartlett's Familiar Quotations: Fourteenth Edition* (Boston: Little, Brown and Company, 1968), p. 966.
2. Lucy S. Dawidowicz, *The War Against the Jews: 1933–1945* (New York: Holt, Rinehart and Winston, 1975), p. 403.
3. Joseph E. Persico, *Nuremberg: Infamy on Trial* (New York: Viking, 1994), p. 441.
4. Deborah Lipstadt, *Denying the Holocaust: The Growing Assault on Truth and Memory* (New York: The Free Press: A Division of Macmillan, Inc., 1993), p. 214.
5. George Santayana, *The Life of Reason,* from *Dictionary of Quotations* (New York: Chambers, 1997), p. 842.
6. Donald S. Detwiler, *Germany: A Short History* (Carbondale, IL: Southern Illinois University Press [revised paperback edition], 1989), p. 171.
7. Whitney R. Harris, *Tyranny on Trial: The Evidence at Nuremberg* (New York: Barnes & Noble Books, 1995), p. 290.
8. Ibid., pp. 290–291.
9. William L. Shirer, *The Rise and Fall of the Third Reich: A History of Nazi Germany* (New York: Simon & Schuster, 1960), p. 964.
10. Daniel Jonah Goldhagen, *Hitler's Willing Executioners: Ordinary Germans and the Holocaust* (New York: Alfred A. Knopf, 1996), p. 149.
11. A. R. Butz, *The Hoax of the Twentieth Century* (Richmond, Surrey, England: Historical Review Press, 1976), Cover Title.

Chapter Two

1. Commentary in *National Review*, September 10, 1971, p. 979.
2. D. D. Gutenplan, *Is a Holocaust Skeptic Fit to Be a Historian,* in *The New York Times,* June 26, 1999, p. B9.
3. Deborah Lipstadt, *Denying the Holocaust: The Growing Assault on Truth and Memory* (New York: The Free Press: A Division of Macmillan, Inc., 1993), p. 161.

4. Sarah Lyall, *London Trial Opens Dispute on Rewriting the Holocaust,* in *The New York Times,* January 12, 2000, p. A7.

5. ————, *Critic of a Holocaust Denier Is Cleared in British Libel Suit,* in *The New York Times,* April 12, 2000, pp. A1 and A6.

6. Gutenplan, pp. B9 and B11.

7. Ibid., p. 11.

8. Lyall, *Critic of a Holocaust Denier,* p. A6.

9. Mark Weber, *My Role in the Zundel Trial,* from *The Journal of Historical Review*, vol. 9, no. 4, pp. 389–425. Internet: http://www.ihr.org/jhr/v09/v09p389_Weber.html

10. Institute of Historical Review, *Newsletter,* October 1988, p. 7.

11. Lipstadt, pp. 144–145.

12. Ibid., p. 144.

13. Ibid., pp. 144–145.

14. Lucy S. Dawidowicz, *The War Against the Jews: 1933–1945* (New York: Holt, Rinehart and Winston, 1975), p. 91.

15. Ibid.

16. Ibid., p. 92.

17. A. R. Butz, *The Hoax of the Twentieth Century* (Richmond, Surrey, England: Historical Review Press, 1976), p. 68.

18. Ibid., p. 11.

19. Lipstadt, p. 125.

Chapter Three

1. Alan Bullock, *Hitler and Stalin: Parallel Lives* (New York: Alfred A. Knopf, 1992), p. 595. From *The Testament of Adolph Hitler: The Hitler Bormann Documents* (English translation, London: 1961), p. 66.

2. Deborah Lipstadt, *Denying the Holocaust: The Growing Assault on Truth and Memory* (New York: The Free Press: A Division of Macmillan, Inc., 1993), p. 47.

3. Bullock, p. 23.

4. *Chronicles of the 20th Century* (Mount Kisco, NY: Chronicle Publications, 1987), p. 419.

5. William L. Shirer, *The Rise and Fall of the Third Reich: A History of Nazi Germany* (New York: Simon & Schuster, 1960), p. 964.

6. Bullock, p. 759.

7. Anonymous. *Holocaust Denial: Bigotry in the Guise of Scholarship* (Los Angeles: Simon Wiesenthal Center Report, 1994), p. 23.

8. Paul Kuttner, *The Holocaust: Hoax or History?* (New York: Dawnwood Press, 1996), p. 72.

9. Ibid., p. 99.

10. *Encyclopedia of the Holocaust,* vol. 2 (New York: 1990), pp. 105–106.

11. Bullock, p. 762.

12. Kuttner, p. 98.

13. *Newsletter of the National Socialist White American Party,* March 1991.

14. Arthur R. Butz, *A short introduction to the study of Holocaust revisionism,* May 5, 1998. Internet: http://pubweb.acns.nwu.edu/~abutz/di/intro.html

15. Ibid.

16. A. R. Butz, *The Hoax of the Twentieth Century* (Richmond, Surrey, England: Historical Review Press, 1976), p. 237.

17. Institute of Historical Review: *A Revisionist Perspective: 66 Questions and Answers on the Holocaust.* Internet: http://www.ihr.org/leaflets/66qna.html

18. Anne Frank, *The Diary of a Young Girl* (New York: Bantam Books [paperback], 1993), p. 208.

Chapter Four

1. Austin App, *The Six Million Swindle: Blackmailing the German People for Hard Marks with Fabricated Corpses* (Tacoma Park, MD, 1973), pp. 18–19.

2. Whitney R. Harris, *Tyranny on Trial: The Evidence at Nuremberg* (New York: Barnes & Noble Books, 1995), pp. 336–337.

3. Mark Weber, *The Holocaust: Let's hear both sides.* Internet: http://www.ihr.org/leaflets/both sides.html

4. Institute of Historical Review: *A Revisionist Perspective: 66 Questions and Answers on the Holocaust.* Internet: http://www.ihr.org/leaflets/66qna.html

5. William L. Shirer, *The Rise and Fall of the Third Reich: A History of Nazi Germany* (New York: Simon & Schuster, 1960), p. 971.

6. Institute of Historical Review.

7. Deborah Lipstadt, *Denying the Holocaust: The Growing Assault on Truth and Memory* (New York: The Free Press: A Division of Macmillan, Inc., 1993), p. 137.

8. *Shofar FTP Archive File:* Internet: people/m/mermelstein.mel/mermelstein.text

9. *Mr. Death: The Rise and Fall of Fred A. Leuchter Jr.,* A Film Review by James Berardinelli. Internet: http://movie-reviews.colossus.net/movies/m/mr_death.html

10. Lipstadt, p. 165.

11. The Nizkor Project: *The Leuchter Report: Overview.* Internet: http://mindit.netmind.com/proxy/http://www.nizkor.org/faqs/leuchter/leuchter-faq-02.html

12. The Nizkor Project: *The Leuchter Report: Disparities in Hydrocyanic Compound Levels.* Internet: http://mindit.netmind.com/proxy/http://www.nizkor.org/faqs/leuchter/leuchter-faq-04.html

13. The Nizkor Project: *The Leuchter Report: The people who dropped . . .* Internet: http://mindit.netmind.com/proxy/http://www.nizkor.org/faqs/leuchter/leuchter-faq-14.html

14. Ibid.

15. The Nizkor Project: *The Leuchter Report: If the gas chambers were ventilated . . .* Internet: http://mindit.netmind.com/proxy/http://www.nizkor.org/faqs/leuchter/leuchter-faq-12.html

16. Ibid.

17. The Nizkor Project: *The Leuchter Report: Gas chambers could not have been opened safely . . .* Internet: http://mindit.netmind.com/proxy/http://www.nizkor.org/faqs/leuchter/leuchter-faq-06.html

18. The Nizkor Project: *The Leuchter Report: The "extermination" chambers were actually morgues.*

Internet: http://mindit.netmind.com/proxy/http://www.nizkor.org/faqs/leuchter/leuchter-faq-07.html

19. The Nizkor Project: *The Leuchter Report: Doors of gas chambers too weak to prevent escape.* Internet: http://mindit.netmind.com/proxy/http://www.nizkor.org/faqs/leuchter/leuchter-faq-09.html

20. The Nizkor Project: *The Leuchter Report: If so many people . . .* Internet: http://mindit.netmind.com/proxy/http://www.nizkor.org/faqs/leuchter/leuchter-faq-13.html

21. Ibid.

Chapter Five

1. Author Anonymous, *The encampment of the Jews: Might it have been justified?* Internet: http://www.corax.org/revisionism/misc/encampment.html

2. *Encyclopaedia Britannica,* vol. III (Chicago: Encyclopaedia Britannica, Inc., 1984), p. 60.

3. William L. Shirer, *The Rise and Fall of the Third Reich: A History of Nazi Germany* (New York: Simon & Schuster, 1960), p. 952.

4. *Chronicle of the 20th Century* (Mount Kisco, NY: Chronicle Publications, 1987), p. 33.

5. Institute of Historical Review: *A Revisionist Perspective: 66 Questions and Answers on the Holocaust.* Internet: www.ihr.org/leaflets/66qna.html

6. Ibid.

7. Author anonymous.

8. Lucy S. Dawidowicz, *The War Against the Jews: 1933–1945* (New York: Holt, Rinehart and Winston, 1975), pp. 374 and 403.

9. Pierre Vidal-Naquet, *Assassins of Memory: Essays on the Denial of the Holocaust* (New York: Columbia University Press, 1992), p. 16.

10. Blanche Wiesen Cook*, Eleanor Roosevelt: Volume 2, 1933–1938* (New York: Viking, 1999), p. 441.

11. Ted Gottfried, *Enrico Fermi: Pioneer of the Atomic Age* (New York: Facts on File, 1992), p. 105.

Chapter Six

1. Whitney H. Harris, *Tyranny On Trial: The Evidence at Nuremberg* (New York: Barnes & Noble Books, 1995), p. 310.

2. Ibid., p. 393.

3. Ibid., pp. 402–403.

4. Ibid., p. 404.

5. Nomi Morris, "On the Trail of Looted Art," *Macleans,* July 27, 1998, pp. 48–51.

6. Dr. William Pierce, *The Holocaust Shakedown,* on the Adelaide Institute Newsletter 86, January 1999. Internet:
http://www.adam.com.au/fredadin/newsletters/news86.html

7. *Chronicle of the 20th Century* (Mount Kisco, NY: Chronicle Publications, 1987), p. 705.

8. Austin App, *The Six Million Swindle: Blackmailing the German People for Hard Marks with Fabricated Corpses* (Tacoma Park, MD: self-published, 1973), p. 2.

9. Harry Elmer Barnes, *Zionist Fraud,* an appendix to *The Myth of the Six Million* (Los Angeles: Noontide Press, 1969), p. 37.

10. N. Sagi, *German Reparations: A History of the Negotiations* (Jerusalem: Magnes Press, 1980), p. 55.

11. Hannah Arendt, *Eichmann in Jerusalem: A Report on the Banality of Evil* (New York: Penguin Books [paperback], 1994), p. 79.

12. The Nizkor Project: *Shofar FTP Archive File.*
    Internet: www.nizkor.org/ftp.cgi/people/z/zundel.ernst/zundelgrams/1997/zgram970102

13. Germany Alert, October 28, 1999, *Swiss Rightwing Wins.*
    Internet: www.antiracist.com/breaking/swiss/shtml

14. Professor Harry Elmer Barnes, Ph.D., quoted in *War Crimes Trials.*
    Internet: www.corax.org/revisionism/misc/ar/trials.html

Chapter Seven

1. Article [I] of the Bill of Rights (the First Amendment to the United States Constitution), *Encyclopaedia Britannica,* vol. X (Chicago: Encyclopaedia Britannica, Inc., 1984), p. 1045.

2. Valerie Curry Bradley, *Cyberhate and the First Amendment,* pp. 2–3.
   Internet: http://wings.buffalo.edu/law/Complaw/CompLawPapers/bradley.html

3. Oliver Wendell Holmes, Jr., *United States* v. *Schwimmer [1928]* in *Bartlett's Familiar Quotations: Fourteenth Edition* (Boston: Little, Brown and Company, 1968), p. 789 a.

4. Bradley, p. 5.

5. Howard Berkowitz for the Anti-Defamation League on *Hate on the Internet* before the Senate Committee on the Judiciary, September 14, 1999.
   Internet: http://www.senate.gov/~judiciary/91499ad.htm

6. Ibid.

7. Adolf Hitler, *Mein Kampf,* vol. 1, Ch. 6, in *Bartlett's Familiar Quotations: Fourteenth Edition* (Boston: Little, Brown and Company, 1968), p. 1012.

8. Berkowitz.

9. Author anonymous, *Restrict Hate Speech on Internet.*
   Internet: http://www.district94.dupage.k12.il.us/social_studies/gov_spring-00/realbill_text.htm

10. Author anonymous, *Facing the First Amendment Future* (A First Amendment Summit sponsored by The Freedom Forum First Amendment Center at Vanderbilt University).
    Internet: http://www.fac.org/publicat/fafuture.htm

11. Pamela Mandels, *Rights Group Develops "Hate" Filter,* from *The New York Times on the Web,* November 11, 1998.
    Internet: www.nytimes.com/library/tech/98/11/cyber/articles/12filter.html

12. Charles W. Moore, *Thin Edge of the Wedge: Why Internet Censorship Is a Bad Idea,* on *MacMall News Site.*
    Internet: www.mactimes.com/features/maccave51799.shtml

13. Author anonymous, *Censorship vs. Freedom of Speech; The Case of Hate Speech on the Net.* Internet: mainline.brynmawr.edu/~ccongdon/cs110spring98/Webpapers/hussain.html
14. Ibid.
15. Mandels.
16. Elizabeth G. Olson, *More on the UN Internet Hate Speech Conference,* from *The New York Times,* November 24, 1997. Internet: www.nytimes.com/library/cyber/week/112497racism.html or www.pili.org/lists/piln/archives/msg00107.html
17. Daniel A. Tyvser (Beck & Tyvser), *Germany Indicts Compuserve Official.* Internet: www.bitlaw.com/hot/bavaria.html
18. Rick Goldberg: *Religion in the Technological Age: Dealing with Anti-Semitism on the Internet.* Internet: http://yucc.yorku.ca/~rickg/academics/hatenet.html

Chapter Eight

1. Plato, *Dialogues, Phaedo, 91* in *Bartlett's Familiar Quotations: Fourteenth Edition* (Boston: Little, Brown and Company, 1968), p. 93.
2. Jonathan Dube, *Furrow in Custody.* Internet: ABCNEWS.com
3. Carolyn Tuft and Joe Holleman, *The FBI Calls It the Nation's Most Dangerous Hate Group,* in the *St. Louis Post-Dispatch,* March 5, 2000, p. A1.
4. Jason Epstein and Eric Rozenman, *Buford O. Furrow, Jr. North Valley Community Center Shooting Suspect,* in the *B'nai B'rith News.* Internet: bnaibrith.org/pr/furrow81699.html
5. Kia Shante Breaux, *Hate Group's Author in Spotlight,* from *The Associated Press* on the World Council of Independent Churches Web page. Internet: www.wcicc.org/news/general/24.html
6. Tuft and Holleman.
7. Anonymous, *Talk Radio Assassination: Alan Berg,* Internet:www.wfmu.org/LCD/GreatDJ/berg.html
8. Karen Brandon and Michael J. Berens, *Hate Groups Using Recent Violence as Recruitment Tool* in the *Buffalo News,* August 22, 1999, p. H5.
9. Anonymous, *Phineas Priests Arrested in Spokane Robberies,* in the *Montana Human Rights Network News,* October 1996. Internet: www.mhrn.org/news/1096phin.html
10. Jim Nesbitt, *Mixing the Bible With Bullets,* in the *Denver Post,* August 22, 1999, p. H-06.
11. Deputy Larry Richards, *Domestic Terrorism: Phineas Priests* in *Police and Security News.* Internet: eob.org/terror/html/phineas-priesthood.html
12. Anonymous, *Phineas Priests Arrested . . .*
13. Brandon and Berens.
14. Richard Marosi and Jason Kandel, *Nazi Gang Called Key Player in Drug Trade,* in *The Los Angeles Times,* August 20, 1999, p. 1.
15. Ibid.
16. Ibid.
17. Ibid.
18. Robert S. Wistrich, *Haider and His Critics,* in *Commentary,* April 2000, pp. 30–31.
19. *Chronicle of the 20th Century* (Mount Kisco, NY: Chronicle Publications, 1987), p. 1278.

20. Ibid., p. 1283.
21. Wistrich.
22. Roger Cohen, *Hitler Apologist Wins German Honor, and a Storm Breaks Out,* in *The New York Times,* June 21, 2000, p. A3.
23. Michael Shermer and Alex Grobman, *Denying History* (Los Angeles: University of California Press, 2000), p. 10.

Afterword

1. Anonymous, *The Apocrypha, I Esdras, 4:41* in *Bartlett's Familiar Quotations: Fourteenth Edition* (Boston: Little, Brown and Company, 1968), p. 36.
2. Ursula Duba, *Tales From a Child of the Enemy* (New York: Penguin Books [paperback], 1997), p. 153.

GLOSSARY

anti-Semitism—irrational hatred and persecution of Jews

Auschwitz—Nazi death camp in Poland where approximately 2.5 million Jews were murdered

concentration camp—place of confinement for anti-Nazis and Jews; workplace; slaughterhouse

crematoriums—ovens disposing of the bodies of those gassed in the death camps

Death Books—daily records kept by Nazis of mass executions in death camps

death camps—those concentration camps equipped for mass killing

Final Solution—the Nazi plan to kill off the entire Jewish population of Europe

genocide—the killing of a whole race, people, or nation

ghetto—a confined area in which Jews were forced to live

Holocaust—the systematic extermination of 6 million European Jews by the Nazis

Judenrein—Literally, "rid of Jews," as in Hitler's stated policy to rid Europe of all Jews

Kristallnacht—"Night of Broken Glass" in 1938 when Jewish shops, homes, and synagogues were smashed by Nazis with encouragement from the authorities

Ku Klux Klan—an antiblack, anti-Jewish, anti-Catholic organization with an extensive history of violence

leaderless resistance—a technique for remaining anonymous while committing acts of bigotry and violence

National Socialism—the anti-Semitic political party of Nazis and neo-Nazis

National Socialist White People's Party—a prominent neo-Nazi organization

Nuremberg trials—the trials of Nazi war criminals for crimes against humanity conducted by an international tribunal

Phineas Priests—anti-Semitic white supremacists who advocate and commit violent acts, including robbery and murder

The Protocols of the Learned Elders of Zion—1897 document forged by Russian secret police to foment violence against Jews

reparations—money paid by those responsible to victims of the Nazis and/or their families

revisionism—legitimately, the reinterpretation of historical facts; as used by anti-Semites, it is a term used without factual basis to question the reality of the Holocaust

Sonderkommandos—Jewish death camp prisoners assigned to disposing of the corpses of victims

Wannsee Conference— meeting of Nazi leaders in 1942 to plan how to kill Jews more efficiently

Zyklon-B—the crystals used to make the gas uscd for mass killings during the Holocaust

FOR MORE INFORMATION

Browning, Christopher, R. *Ordinary Men: Reserve Police Battalion 101 and the Final Solution in Poland.* New York: HarperCollins Publishers, 1992.

Dawidowicz, Lucy S. *The War Against the Jews: 1933–1945.* New York: Holt, Rinehart and Winston, 1975.

Duba, Ursula. *Tales From a Child of the Enemy.* New York: Penguin Books [paperback], 1997.

Frank, Anne. *The Diary of a Young Girl.* New York: Bantam Books [paperback], 1993.

Goldhagen, Daniel Jonah. *Hitler's Willing Executioners: Ordinary Germans and the Holocaust.* New York: Alfred A. Knopf, 1996.

Lipstadt, Deborah. *Denying the Holocaust: The Growing Assault on Truth and Memory.* New York: The Free Press: A Division of Macmillan, Inc., 1993.

Shermer, Michael, and Alex Grobman. *Denying History.* Los Angeles: University of California Press, 2000.

Shirer, William L. *The Rise and Fall of the Third Reich: A History of Nazi Germany.* New York: Simon & Schuster, 1960.

Spiegelman, Art. *Maus: A Survivor's Tale: My Father Bleeds History.* New York: Pantheon Books [paperback], 1986.

———. *Maus II: A Survivor's Tale: And Here My Troubles Begin.* New York: Pantheon Books, 1991.

Vidal-Naquet, Pierre. *Assassins of Memory: Essays on the Denial of the Holocaust.* New York: Columbia University Press, 1992.

Recommended Films

Mr. Death: The Rise and Fall of Fred A. Leuchter Jr. (documentary), directed by Errol Morris.

Schindler's List, directed by Steven Spielberg, 1993.

Shoah (French documentary), directed by Claude Lanzmann, *1985.*

Internet Sites

Anti-Defamation League
www.adl.org/

Germany Alert: The Free Flow of Uncensored Facts
germanyalert.com

The Holocaust: an Historical Summary
www.ushmm.org/education/history.html

Holocaust Resources on the World Wide Web
http://www.fred.net/nhhs/html/hololink.htm

The Jewish Student Online Research Center (Jsource)
www.us-israel.org/jsource/

Lawstreet Journal
www.lawstreet.com/journal/art000112hate.html

The Nizkor Project
www.nizkor.org

Remembering the Holocaust
yarra.vicnet.net.au/~aragorn/holocaus.htm

Shofar FTP Archive Directory
www.nizkor.org/ftp.cgi

Steven Spielberg Jewish Film Archive
www.sites.huji.ac.il/jfa/jfavid.htm

The United States Holocaust Memorial Museum
www.ushmm.org/

INDEX

Page numbers in *italics* refer to illustrations.

Adenauer, Konrad, 72
American Civil Liberties Union (ACLU), 83, 86
American Revolution, 57–58
Anti-Defamation League (ADL), 28, 80, 82, 83, 93
Anti-Semitism, 13, 15, 31, 80, 89
    evolution of German policy of, 18–19
    hate groups, 89–91
    history of, 15–17
    of Hitler, 34–36
    on Internet hate sites, 80, 84
    language of, 15
App, Austin J., 44, 45
Art work, 69–70, *71*
Aryan Nation, 90, 91
Aryan Republican Army (ARA), 92
Atomic bombs, 64, *65*, 66, 91
Auschwitz concentration camp, 24, 41, 45, 48–53
Austria, 94–96

Beckwith, Byron de la, 92
Belsen concentration camp, 41
Berg, Alan, 90
Bigotry, language of, 13, 15
Birkenau concentration camp, 50
Black Americans, 62–64, 81, 93
Blocher, Christoph, 74

Boer War concentration camps, 59
Braque, Georges, 10
British prison ships, 58
Buckley, William, 29
Buhler, Joseph, 36
Butz, A. R., 30–31

Carto, Willis, 22, 28–30
Center for Democratic Renewal (CDR), 93, 94
Chaney, James E., 63
Christian Identity, 90, 91
Churchill, Winston, 28
Civil War, 62, 81
Communications Decency Act of 1996, 85
Covington, Harold, 81
Craig, Gordon, 25
Cyber Patrol, 83

"Death Books," 12
Delamuraz, Jean-Pascal, 74
Denying the Holocaust: The Growing Assault on Truth and Memory (Lipstadt), 24
Destruction of the European Jews, The (Hilberg), 24
Diary of Anne Frank, The, 39, *40*, 41–42
Didier Works, 48
Did Six Million Really Die? (pub. Zundel), 26
Dietz, George, 25

Diseases, 38–39, 41
Duba, Ursula, 100

Eichmann, Adolf, 36–37
Eisenhower, Dwight, 66
Evers, Medgar, 92

Faurisson, Robert, 98
Feinstein, Dianne, 83
Felderer, Ditlieb, 26, 28
Final Solution, 11–12, 19–20
First Amendment of the U.S. Constitution, 78, 79, 83, 85, 86
Fish, Hamilton, 63
Focal Point Publications, 50
Frank, Anne, 41–42
Frank, Hans, 36
Furrow, Buford O'Neal, 89–91

Gale, Mary Ellen, 83
Geyer, Michael, 25
Ghettos, 15–17
Goebbels, Joseph, 36
Goebbels, Mastermind of the Third Reich (Irving), 24
Gold, 73
Goodman, Andrew, 63
Göring, Hermann, 19, 69, 70
Graf, Jurgen, 74
Gray, Charles, 25
Gutherie, Richard Lee, 92

Haider, Jorg, 95–96, *97*
Hale, Matthew, 92–93